A
Price Guide
to
COOKBOOKS
and
RECIPE LEAFLETS

Linda J. Dickinson

COLLECTOR BOOKS
A Division of Schroeder Publishing Co., Inc.

The current values in this book should be used only as a guide. They are not intended to set prices, which vary from one section of the country to another. Auction prices as well as dealer prices vary greatly and are affected by condition as well as demand. Neither the Author nor the Publisher assumes responsibility for any losses that might be incurred as a result of consulting this guide.

DEDICATION

To my mother,
who tossed the first box of cookbooks at me to price for her
which was the inspiration for this book.

INTRODUCTION

Cookbooks have been around for hundreds of years. The earliest inscriptions of recipes were found scrawled on fireplaces and kitchen walls in the ruins of Pompeii after the eruption of Mt. Vesuvius in 79 A.D.

Nearly 2,000 years ago, recipes were being collected and recorded. Marcus Gavius Apicius authored the first written books on cookery. His manuscript *De re conquinaria* dates to the 9th century when Emperor Tiberius reigned. The first traceable printed cookbook, *De Honesta Voluptate*, dates to about 1475. The earliest cookbook printed in English was *The Boke of Cokery* written by R. Pynson during the 1500's. Let's assume, however, that you can't find any of these books, and we will jump to the earliest American cookbook. That was the *Complete Housewife*, edited by Wm. Parks in 1742. It was merely a reprint of an earlier English book. Amelia Simmons wrote *American Cookery* in 1796, the first cookbook actually written in America.

From 1824 to 1854, Eliza Leslie wrote many books, making her the leading American cookbook writer of her time. The first authentic regional cookbook, *Virgina Housewife*, was written by Mary Randolph in 1824.

Cookbooks were primarily in the hands of the professional cooks until the end of the 18th century. Even at this time, recipes were confusing. Often they contained unclear directions and imprecise measurements.

One book I have from 1891 has a recipe for Blackbird Pie - "for a medium size baking dish about four and twenty black birds will be required." Perhaps your medium size pans are bigger than mine!

American women needed better instruction and the 1880's brought scientific cooking to the United States in the form of cooking schools. They seemed to pop up everywhere. Juliet Corson founded the N.Y. Cooking School in 1874. Maria Parloa, Johanna Sweeney and Mary Johnson Baily Lincoln opened schools in Boston. The Philadelphia School of Domestic Science was opened by Sarah Rorer in 1884.

At last printed textbooks and cookbooks containing exact directions and standardized measurements were available to the typical American home-maker.

Fannie Merritt Farmer, born March 23, 1857, was another of these predominant textbook writers. She enrolled in the Boston Cooking School and was such an apt student that after graduation in 1889, she was asked to serve as its assistant director. She held this position until 1891 when she became director. In 1902, she resigned and opened her own school known as Miss Farmer's School of Cookery. The first of her books was *Boston Cooking School Cookbook*. It was handwritten and in 1896, when she submitted it to the publisher, Little Brown & Co., Miss Farmer had to pay for publishing the first 3,000 copies because her publishers didn't think it would be successful. It has sold over one million copies.

On the death of Miss Farmer in 1915, her cookbook was taken over by her sister. After the passing of her sister, the task fell to Wilma Perkins, her daughter-in-law. Wilma Perkins lived in Rochester, NY. She saw the book through seven revisions, beginning in 1929. This book was the standard in cookbooks until *The Joy of Cooking* took over. She also wrote *The Fannie Farmer Junior Cookbook*. Miss Farmer's cookbook is the longest lived cookbook and is still being published by Little Brown & Co.

The *Settlement Cookbook* was also a bestseller; it sold one million copies. Others selling over a million include *Fannie Farmer's Cookbook, Joy of Cooking, Good Housekeeping, McCall's Cookbook and Betty Crocker's Cookbook.* However, the *Better Homes and Gardens New Cookbook* holds the sales record; it has sold over 18 million copies.

Cookbooks first appeared in the antique and collectible price guides in the early 1980's. Since then, the prices have been going up rapidly and erratically. Everyone is trying to find the right selling price. Many dealers don't know what they are selling or who is buying. Each is trying to zero in on a fair selling price.

Understanding the cookbook buyers seems to be the real key to this collectible. Perhaps if I tell you of a few examples of those I have sold it might better help you to understand. This past spring I sold a small recipe leaflet, ca. 1930. It was rather undesirable to my eye. The back page was stained, it had a few mediocre recipes, and no known author or advertiser. The first time I put it out for sale, it was whisked away at $5.00. I inquired why this lady was buying it and if she was a cookbook collector. The response was "No, but my friend collects anything with the Statue of Liberty on it." Well, the cover did have a rather simple but nice print of the Statue of Liberty. This made me pull back and reassess cookbook collectors. Immediately, I found that paper books and leaflets with attractive covers were a very big part of the market. St. Nicholas Flour leaflets with Santa on the cover were in demand by antiquers who decorate at the holidays with old ornaments and such. Jewel Tea collectors wanted the matching cookbook. Collectors of celebrity memorabilia snatched up Kate Smith and Yul Brynner. Brewery people grabbed the 7-up recipe flyers and so on. All demanded cookbooks in good condition, especially the covers.

Recently I met a young woman who owns a local farm market. In her shop, she was actively selling old cookbooks for - of all things - the recipes! Suddenly, ladies knew that the best recipes were in the old books, on the bottom of the pile, that were held together with tape and rubberbands, covered with stains, and the back covers slightly baked. The same ladies favored loose pages. I wondered what kind of cookbooks were left without a home. When the call came, "I want all the local church and women's club cookbooks you can find for our area," I knew no cookbook would ever be an orphan; it just needed to be matched to the correct owner. So many have been published for so many years that this price guide could go on for miles.

I'm hoping that you will use this introduction to help guide you in pricing the thousands you'll find not listed here. These prices reflect actual sales within recent months in our area. I've included some newer books I feel will develop a market in the future. I expect titles will be an area to watch out for. The titles conjured up in the 1960's, 1970's and 1980's are bound to develop their own markets more for social attitudes and historical

5

reasons than for content. *Cooking in the Nude* has to make some kind of statement as does *The Benevolent Bean* and *Entertaining with Insects*.

When pricing a cookbook, consider the group to which it will be most appealing - recipe users, World's Fair people, for the cover, advertising, children's books, etc. Next compare it to similar ones I've listed. Look at hard cover, paperback, number of pages, condition, cover, and age.

Please realize also that prices in the areas I surveyed are low. Commonly, dealers consider our area about 20% lower than most price guides on the market, so not bumping these prices slightly for large cities might be a mistake.

With cookbooks still being discovered, prices will continue to fluctuate until standardized by buyers and sellers everywhere. Thanks to all you cookbook collectors and dealers who have provided a need for this book. I hope it will help you.

KEY TO
PRICE GUIDE ABBREVIATIONS

env .... envelope
hb .... hard bound
lf .... leaflet
pb .... paper back
pp .... pages
sgn .... signed

A
Price Guide
to
COOKBOOKS
and
RECIPE LEAFLETS

NUMERALS

3 Meals a Day
Metro Life, 16 pp, lf...**$2.00**

3 Stalks of Corn
L. Politi, 1908...**$18.00**

9 Famous Recipes
Hershey, 1956, lf...**$1.00**

10 Cakes Husbands Like Best
Spry, 16 pp, (Aunt Jenny inside)...**$2.00**

13 Colonies Cookbook
A. Donovan, 1975, 270 pp, hb **$8.00**

18 Unusual Recipes
Jack Frost Sugar, 1930, pb **$2.00**

20 Lessons in Domestic Science
Calmut, 1915, 108 pp **$7.00**

20th Century Cookbook
M. Cooke, 1897, 608 pp, hb **$35.00**

20 Wonderful Cakes
Kraft Oil, 1955, lf..**$2.00**

24 Ways to use Log Cabin Syrup
Recipe cards **$20.00**

27 New Recipes for Wilson's Cert. Sliced Bacon
1934 ....**$1.50**

30 New Recipes from the $20,000 Cookbook
Minute Tapioca, 1929, 20 pp, pb...**$2.50**

30 New Recipes,
Minute Tapioca, 1929, 20 pp, lf...**$1.50**

32 Better Barbecues
Feindold, 1983, 63 pp **$2.00**

40 Tested Recipes
Short, Best Foods, 1927, 16 pp, pb...**$3.00**

48 Meat Extending Recipes
D. Stuart, 22 pp, pb **$2.50**

48 Tasty Recipes Made with Sunshine Pimento
Pomona Products, 15 pp, lf **$1.50**

50 Alltime Great Hamburger Recipes
Betty Crocker, 15 pp, lf ....**$ .75**

50 Good Ways to Serve Woodcock Macaroni
1919, 50 pp, lf **$5.00**

50 Years of Bounty at Mt. Olive
1972, 252 pp, pb **$5.00**

51 Pancake Recipes from the 1967 Mrs. America Pageant
52 pp, lf...**$3.00**

52 Sunday Dinners
E. Hiller, 1915 ....**$15.00**

52 Sunday Dinners
Woman's World Magazine, 1927, 66 pp **$6.00**

55 Ways to Save Eggs
Royal Baking, 1917, 22 pp, pb $3.00

60 Minute Chef
1947, Truax, 222 pp $5.00

60th Anniversary, Ladies Village Improvement Society, NY
1960, 65 pp $7.50

60 Ways to Serve Armour Star Ham
31 pp, pb $2.00

65 Delicious Dishes Made with Bread
Fleishmann, 1919 .... $10.00

69 Rations Recipes for Meat
M. Giffords, 29 pp $3.50

75 of Seasoning Secrets
Gulden Co., 1952, 21 pp, pb $2.00

75 Recipes for Pastry, Cakes & Sweetmeats
Leslie, 1835 .... $85.00

77 Recipes Using Swift'ning
M. Logan, 1950, 35 pp, pb $3.00

99 Tempting Pineapple Treats
Libby, 1925, 32 pp $3.00

100 Centennial Recipes
Flour Mills Texas Centennial Expo, 1936, 32 pp, pb $3.50

100 Delights
Hills Bros., 1924, 31 pp, pb $4.50

100 Glorified Recipes
Carnation Milk, 1930, pb $3.00

100 Glorified Recipes
M. Blake, 1933, 36pp, lf $1.25

100 Shefford Cheese Recipes
1938, 36 pp, lf $2.00

100 Special Receipts
Dr. Chase, 32 pp, pb $3.00

100 Tested Crisco Recipes
Crisco, 1906, pb $5.50

100 Ways to Serve Armour
1934, 51 pp, lf $2.50

101 All-Time Favorite Cranberry Recipes
Ocean Spray, 36 pp $2.00

108 Sensible Recipes
Bakers Extract, 1921, env $4.00

133 Quicker Ways to Homemade . . . Bisquick
Crocker, 1959, 27 pp, pb $2.50

146 Adventures in Beef Cookery
Swift, 1958, 98 pp, pb $2.00

150 Rec. Casserole Cookery
Tracey, 1943, 154 pp, hb $2.00

159 Exciting Meals to do with Sausage
I. Allen, 1957, 48 pp, pb $2.00

100 Shefford Cheese Recipes
By Alberta Winthrop
Copyright 1938 Shefford Cheese Co., Inc.

101 All-Time Favorite Cranberry Recipes
Published by Ocean Spray Cranberry Kitchen

200 Dishes for Men to Cook
A. Deute, 1944, 254 pp **$5.00**
200 Tested Recipes
Crisco, Allen, 80 pp, pb **$4.00**
201 Tasty Dishes for Reducers
V. Lindlahr, 1950, 128 pp, pb..**$2.00**
219 Ways to a Man's Heart
Dane, 76 pp **$3.00**
300 Sugar Saving Recipes
H. Hester, 1908, 181 pp **$6.00**
300 Sugar Saving Recipes
H. Hester, 1942, 181 pp **$6.00**
365 Ways to Cook Hamburger
D. Nickerson, 1960, 189 pp, hb **$5.00**
500 Delicious Salad Recipes
R. Berolzheimer, 1953, 38 pp, lf..**$2.00**
600 Recipes
J. Marquart, 1890, 311 pp, hb **$15.00**
700 Sandwiches
F. Cowles, 1929, 246 pp **$6.00**
1,000 Ways to Please a Husband
Bettina's, 1917, 480 pp, hb **$25.00**
1001 Frozen Food Hints
D. Taylor, 1957, 123 pp **$2.50**
1924, a Jell-O Year
14 pp, pb **$3.00**
1980 Olympic Games in Moscow Cookbook & Schedule
1979, 160 pp, pb **$12.00**
2,000 Useful Facts about Food
1954, pb **$4.50**
10,000 Snacks
Brown, 1948, 593 pp, hb..**$10.00**
200,000 for Breakfast with Tom Breneman
1943, 48 pp **$6.00**

A & P Cookbook
1975, 288 pp **$8.00**
ABC's of Food Freezing
Ben-Hur, 1953, 128 pp, pb **$3.00**
A Date with a Dish, American Negro Recipes
deKnight, 1948, 426 pp **$15.00**
A Few Hints About Cooking
S. Grier, 1887, 319 pp **$30.00**
A Friend in Need, Arm & Hammer
1933, 28 pp, lf **$3.50**
a la Rector, Culinary Mysteries
1933, 110 pp, hb, sgn **$6.00**
A World of Good Eating
Jack Frost, 1951, 128 pp, pb **$6.00**
AAUW Cookbook, Rochester, NY
1969, 585 pp, pb **$5.50**
ABC Casserole
Peter Pauper Press, 1954, 61 pp, pb **$3.50**
ABC of Canapes
R. McCrae, 1953 .... **$3.50**
Adirondack Country Cookbook
Colton, NY, 1987, 206 pp, pb **$5.00**
After 50 Cookbook
D. Hamilton, 1974, 365 pp **$10.00**
Alice B. Toklas Cook Book
1954, 288 pg **$7.00**
Alice Bay Cookbook
J. Rousseau, 1985, 247 pp, pb **$4.00**
Alice Bradley Menu Cookbook
Bradley, 1944, 944 pp **$12.00**
All About Baking
1937, 144 pp, hb **$12.50**
All About Home Baking
General Foods, 1933, 144 pp, hb.. **$5.00**
All About Home Baking
General Foods, 1935, 144 pp, hb.. **$6.00**
All About Meat
Frigidaire, 1953, 31 pp.. **$1.00**
All About Steam Cooking
C. Truax, 1981, 264 pp, hb **$7.50**
All American Cookbook, Favorite Recipes of Famous Persons
1954, 106 pp+, pb **$4.00**
All Electric-mix Recipes
General Mills, pb **$1.00**
All Maine Cooking
R. Wiggin, 1968, 187 pp, pb **$5.50**

A Friend in Need
Arm & Hammer Baking Soda

a la Rector
**"Unveiling the Culinary Mysteries of the world famous
George Rector"**

A World of Good Eating
Recipes From Around The World
Copyright 1951 by Jack Frost Studios

All Maine Cooking
A Collection of Treasured Recipes from The Pine Tree State
A Courier-Gazette Publication

All New Fannie Farmer Cooking School Book
Bantam Books, 1962, 648 pp, hb **$4.00**
All Time Favorite Recipe Salads
1986, 88 pp **$1.00**
All-in-One Calorie Counter
J. Carper, 1974, pb **$5.00**
All-Star Cookbook
Winona Chapter #141, 1922, 201 pp **$10.00**
Alladin's Lamp at Mealtimes
Premier Coffee, 1927, 47 pp, lf... **$1.50**
Alphabet for Gourmets
M. Fisher, 1949, 1st printing **$8.50**
Always Eggs . . . All Ways
American Egg Board, 1974, 33 pp, lf **$1.50**
Amana Recipes
1948 .... **$11.00**
American Heart Association Cookbook
T. Hampson, 1973, 411 pp, hb **$12.00**
America's Cook Book
Home Institute, NY, 1937, 1,006 pp, hb **$16.00**
America's Cookbook
Herald Tribune, 1952, 1,088 pp **$12.00**
American Cookery Magazine
1925-35 issues .... **$3.00 each**
American Cookery
J. Beard, 1972, 877 pp, hb **$30.00**
American Cookery
Simmons, 1798, (sold at auction).. **$22,000.00**
American Cookery
Simmons, 1937 .... **$50.00**
American Cooking
1925, 12 volumes, hb **$95.00**
American Cooking
Brown & Time Life, 1968, 208 pp **$10.00**
American Cooks
Fed. Women's Clubs, 1967, 731 pp **$15.00**
American Domestic Cookbook
Herrick, 1870, 32 pp, lf.. **$6.00**
American Everyday Cookbook
1955, 2,000 pp, hb **$12.00**
American Family Cookbook
Cul Arts, 1st edition **$25.00**
American Family Cookbook
J. Carson, 1898... **$45.00**
American Family Cookbook
L. Wallace, 1949, 831 pp, hb **$16.00**
American Home Cookbook by Ladies of Detroit
1878 .... **$45.00**

America's Cook Book
Compiled by The Home Institute of
The New York Herald Tribune

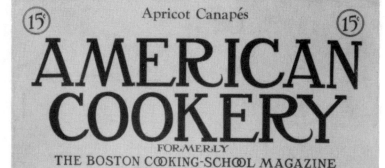

Apricot Canapés

15¢   15¢

AMERICAN COOKERY

FORMERLY

THE BOSTON COOKING-SCHOOL MAGAZINE

APRIL, 1939

VOL. XLIII   No. 9
$1.50 a Year

Easter Appetizers

PUBLISHED
BY
THE BOSTON COOKING-
SCHOOL MAGAZINE C°
221 Columbus Ave
Boston   Mass

American Cookery
Formerly The Boston Cooking School Magazine
April 1939

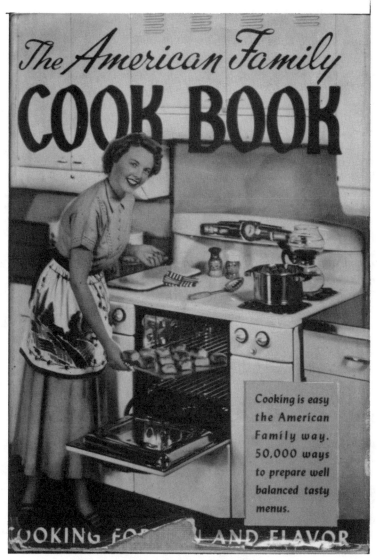

Cooking is easy the American Family way. 50,000 ways to prepare well balanced tasty menus.

The American Family Cook Book
Editor-in-Chief Lily Haxworth Wallace

American Home Cookbook
G. Denison, 1913, 538 pp+ **$10.00**

American Home Cookbook
G. Denison, 1932, 537 pp, hb **$5.50**

American Housewife Cookbook
H. Anners, 1850, 95 pp... **$55.00**

American Pure Foods Cookbook
Sears & Roebuck, 1899 .... **$35.00**

American Regional Cookery
S. Hibbon, 1946, 354 pp, hb **$17.50**

American Regional Cookery
S. Hibbon, 1963, 318 pp **$6.50**

American Way of Progress
Kraft, NY World's Fair, 1939, 20 pp, lf **$5.00**

American Woman's Cookbook
R. Berolzheimer, 1939, 815 pp... **$25.00**

American Woman's Home
C. Beecher, 1869 .... **$75.00**

Ames Woman's Iowa Cookbook
1930 .... **$5.00**

Amy Vanderbilt's Complete Cookbook
1961, 765 pp **$12.00**

An Emblem of Purity
Dove Molasses (DBM kisses last rec), lf **$2.00**

An Epicures Book of Cheese Recipes
J. Rosebrook, 1931, 66 pp... **$2.00**

An Herb and Spice Cookbook
C. Clairborne, 1963, 334 pp **$16.50**

Anatolia College Cookbook; Salonica, Greece
A. Riggs, ca. 1940, 94 pp, pb.. **$5.50**

Ancestral Recipes of Shen Mei Lon
Rosen, 1954, boxed **$4.00**

Angostura Recipes
Black man on cover, lf... **$2.50**

Annemarie's Personnel Cookbook
A. Haust, 1968, 188 pp, pb **$4.00**

Anyone Can Bake
Royal Baking, 1928, 100 pp, hb **$14.00**

Anyone Can Bake
Royal Baking, 1929, 100 pp, hb **$8.00**

Appetizer Book
Good Housekeeping, 1958, 68 pp, hb **$2.00**

Apple-Dore Cook Book
A. Graves, 1872, 234 pp, pb.. **$45.00**

Architecture & Apple Cider
Attica, NY, 1982, 206 pp, pb **$6.00**

Architecture & Maple Syrup
Attica, NY, 1982, 147 pp, pb **$5.00**

An Emblem of Purity
Dove Brand New Orleans Molasses

ANGOSTURA

RECIPES

BRING THE AROMATIC FRAGRANCE OF THE TROPICS TO YOUR TABLE

Angostura Recipes
**Brings The Aromatic Fragrance of the Tropics
to Your Table**

Arm & Hammer Soda
Book of Valuable Recipes
34th Edition
Copyrighted 1900 by Church & Dwight Co., NY.

Arm & Hammer Baking Soda - Good Things to Eat
1930, lf **$5.00**
Arm & Hammer Recipes & Almanac
1896, 32 pp **$15.00**
Arm & Hammer Soda Valuable Recipes
1900, 32 pp, lf **$6.00**
Arm & Hammer Valuable Recipes
1921 ....**$5.00**
Around the World
Good Housekeeping, 1958, 68 pp, pb **$2.00**
Art & Secret of Chinese Cookery
La Choy, 1937, 16 pp, lf **$1.50**
Art of American Indian Cooking
Y. Kimball, 1914-1965, 215 pp **$6.00**
Art of Cookery Made Plain & Easy
Glasse, 1799 ....**$170.00**
Art of Cooking and Serving
Crisco, 1926 ....**$10.00**
Art of Cooking and Serving
Crisco, 1934, 252 pp, pb **$9.50**
Art of Cooking and Serving
Crisco, 1937, 252 pp, pb **$6.50**
Art of Entertaining
Sherwood, 1892 ....**$15.00**
Art of Fine Baking
P. Peck, 1961, 320 pp **$10.00**
Art of Fine Baking
Peck, 1969, 300 pp **$8.00**
Art of French Cooking
F. Garvin, 1962, 170 pp **$3.00**
Art of German Cooking & Baking
L. Meir, 1944, 394 pp **$10.00**
Art of Good Cooking
P. Peck, 1966, 368 pp, pb **$10.00**
Art of Hungarian Cooking
Bennett, 1954, 223 pp, hb **$8.00**
Art of Italian Cooking
M. Pinto, 1948, 177 pp **$6.00**
Art of Italian Cooking
M. Pinto, 1962, 177 pp **$3.00**
Art of Jewish Cooking
J. Grossinger, 1962, 206 pp, pb **$2.00**
Art of Making Bread at Home,
NW Yeast, ca. 1930, 28 pp, black & white cover **$4.00**
Art of Making Good Cookies Plain and Fancy
Ross, 1963, 252 pp **$5.00**
Art of Parisian Cooking
C. Black, 1962, 192 pp, pb **$3.00**

The Art of Making Bread . . . at Home
Northwestern Yeast Co., Chicago, Illinois

Art of Polish Cooking
Zeranska, 1968, 366 pp **$5.00**
Arthritis Cookbook
C. Dong, 1973, 197 pp **$2.50**
Artist in the Kitchen
Memorial Art Gallery, NY, 1960, 385 pp, pb **$10.00**
Arts & Crafts You Can Eat
1974, 127 pp **$2.50**
As the World Cooks
Lowell Mass., 1938, 286 pp **$10.00**
Assist. League Pleasing Food
Calif., ca. 1940, 216 pp **$6.50**
Associated Customer
Lockport Light, NY, 1930, lf **$1.00**
Astor Cookbook
Jane, NY **$30.00**
At Home On The Range
Potter, 1947, 214 pp, hb **$7.00**
Atlanta Woman's Club
1921 .... **$10.00**
Atlas Book of Recipes & Helpful Information on Canning
H. Atlas, ca. 1930 .... **$13.00**
Atlas Book of Recipes
H. Atlas, 1939, 78 pp, pb **$7.00**
Aunt Caroline's Dixieland Recipes
E. McKinney, 1922 .... **$25.00**
Aunt Jane's 50th Anniversary
ca. 1900 .... **$10.00**
Aunt Jane's Cookbook
50 pp **$7.00**
Aunt Jenny's Favorite Recipes
Spry, ca. 1940, 48 pp, pb **$18.00**
Aunt Sammy's Radio Recipes
1927 .... **$3.50**
Aunt Sammy's Rapid Recipes
USDA, 1931, 142 pp **$8.00**
Austrian Cooking
A. Knox, 258 pp **$5.00**
Autumn Leaf
Jewel Tea, 1933 .... **$20.00**

Aunt Jenny's Favorite Recipes
Spry Pure Vegetable Shortening

Baby Epicure
1937, 141 pp, hb **$4.50**
Baccardi Party Book
M. Eckley, 1969, 22 pp, lf **$1.00**
Bake with Bundt
LFP Church, ca. 1970, 20 pp, lf **$2.00**
Baker's Chocolate
1923, pb **$25.00**
Baker's Chocolate
1931, 60 pp **$20.00**
Baker's Cocoa Youth Companion
1915 .... **$20.00**
Baker's Favorite Chocolate Recipes
1950, 112 pp **$5.00**
Baker's Best Chocolate Recipes
1932, lf **$7.00**
Baker's Chocolate Famous Recipes
1928, 63 pp **$4.50**
Baker's Weekly Complete Recipes
C. Glabau, 304 pp **$10.00**
Baking Easy and Delicate
Parker, HP Books, 1982, 240 pp **$7.95**
Baking in a Box - Cooking in a Can
Haines, pb **$3.00**
Balanced Recipes
M. Ames, 1933 .... **$38.00**
Ball Blue Book
Russel, 1930, 56 pp, pb **$15.00**
Ball Canning
1933, lf **$5.00**
Ballet Cookbook
T. Clercq, 1966, 424 pp, hb **$6.00**
Bamberger's Cookbook
McClaire, 1932, 416 pp **$12.00**
Banana Salad Bazaar
Fruit disp. co., ca. 1940, 24 pp **$2.00**
Bar Side Companion
Ed McMahon, 1969, 165 pp **$4.50**
Be an Artist at the Gas Range
Mystery Chef, 1935 .... **$10.00**
Beard on Bread
1976, 230 pp+, hb **$12.00**
Beautiful People's Diet
L. Avedon, 1973, 146 pp, hb **$1.50**
Beginner's Cookbook
Better Homes and Garden, 96 pp **$2.00**

Choice Recipes
Compliments of Walter Baker & Co., Ltd.

Baker's Chocolate, "La Belle Chocolatiére" trademark was from a 1760 painting by Jean-Etienne Liotard, a Swiss painter. Annerl Baltauf, a Viennese girl, died in 1825, but she has graced the Walter Baker Company's packages for years as the Chocolate Girl. The company began in 1780.

Belgian Relief Cookbook
Reading PA, 1915, 317 pp, hb, sgn... **$110.00**
Bell's Spiced Seasoning
1906, lf.. **$2.00**
Benevolent Bean
Keys, 1967, 192 pp, hb **$5.00**
Berks County Cookbook
Pennsylvania Dutch Recipes, ca. 1945, 48 pp, pb **$6.00**
Best Chocolate Recipes
Baker's Chocolate, 1932, 60 pp **$2.00**
Best Foods
1935 .... **$15.00**
Best Loved Foods of Christmas
Pillsbury, 1960, 65 pp, pb... **$4.50**
Best of Bake-off Collection
Pillsbury, 1959 .... **$35.00**
Best of Near Eastern Cookry
A. Seranne, 1964, 158 pp, hb **$6.00**
Best of the Bake-off Recipes
T. Wilson, Australia, 1969, 126 pp, 1st edition **$12.00**
Best Recipes . . . backs of boxes, bottles . . .
C. Dyer, 1979, 194 pp, pb, sgn.. **$4.00**
Best There Is
Ca. 1970, 30 pp, lf.. **$1.00**
Best Wartime Recipes
Royal Baking Powder, 1917, lf... **$2.00**
Best Washington Slug Recipes
(Non-edible) F. Howard, 1983, 32 pp, pb **$2.00**
Bethany Shrine Cookbook
Rochester, NY, 1923, pb.. **$10.00**
Better Cooking
M. Taylor, 15 pp, lf **$2.50**
Better Homes & Garden Cookbook
1939, hb **$15.00**
Better Homes & Garden Cookbook
1953, 414 pp **$10.00**
Better Homes & Garden Cookbook
1968, 160 pp, hb **$10.00**
Better Homes & Garden Junior Cookbook
1972, 80 pp, hb **$4.00**
Better Homes & Garden Lifetime Cookbook
1935 .... **$25.00**
Better Homes & Garden's After Work Cookbook
1974, 112 pp, hb **$4.00**
Better Homes & Garden's Diet Book
1955, 253 pp **$4.00**
Better Homes & Garden's Fondue
1970, 96 pp, hb **$2.00**

My Better Homes & Garden Cookbook
1939

Better Meals for Less Money
H. Young, 1940, 156 pp **$5.00**
Bettina's Best Desserts
L. Weaver, 1923, 194 pp, hb **$20.00**
Bettina's Best Salads & What to . . .
L. Weaver, 1923, 215 pp, hb **$20.00**
Bettina's Cakes and Cookies
L. Weaver, 1924, 224 pp, hb **$20.00**
Betty Crocker All Purpose Baking
1942, 100 pp, pb **$4.00**
Betty Crocker Bisquick Coronation Menu
1 page **$1.00**
Betty Crocker Cookbook
1959, hb **$25.00**
Betty Crocker Dinner for Two
1958, 207 pp, hb, 1st edition **$6.00**
Betty Crocker Dinner for Two
1962, 156 pp **$3.00**
Betty Crocker Dinner in a Dish
1965, 152 pp **$5.00**
Betty Crocker Frankley Fancy Foods
1959, 26 pp, lf **$2.50**
Betty Crocker Good & Easy
1954, small size, 1st edition **$9.00**
Betty Crocker Guide to Easy Entertaining
1959, 178 pp, hb, 1st edition **$10.00**
Betty Crocker Microwave Cookbook
1981, 288 pp, hb **$10.00**
Betty Crocker Picture Cookbook
1956, 472 pp **$20.00**
Betty Crocker's 101 Delicious Biscuit Creations
General Mills, 1933 .... **$3.00**
Betty Crocker Biscuit Cookbook
1971, 124 pp, hb **$6.50**
Betty Furness Westinghouse Cookbook
J. Kiene, 1954, 185 pp **$10.00**
Big Boy Barbecue Book
1957, 54 pp, hb **$6.00**
Billy In Bunbury Cookbook
"Kay," 1925, color **$18.00**
Birds-eye Cookbook
1941, 63 pp, pb **$2.00**
Biscuit & Cakes
Reliable Flour, 1911, 62 pp, lf **$5.00**
Biscuits and Biscuits Glorified
Rumford, 1941, 16 pp **$2.00**
Biscuits for Salads
National Bisuit, 1926, 8 pp, lf **$2.00**

Betty Crocker's Guide to Easy Entertaining
How to Have Guests - And Enjoy Them

Bisquick All Star Cookbook
1935 .... $10.00
Bisquick Cookbook
1964, 112 pp, hb $2.00
Blender Cookbook
Seranne, 1961, 288 pp $6.50
Blender Way to Better Cooking
B. Sullivan, 1965, 208 pp, hb $8.00
Blondie Soup & Sandwich Cookbook
1947 .... $12.00
Blue Book of Cookery
B. Tartan, 1971, 300 pp, hb.................................... $10.00
Blue Moon Recipes
Blue Moon Cheese, 1934, 20 pp, lf $1.50
Blue Ribbon Malt Extract
P. Penny, 1953, 32 pp $5.50
Blue Sea Cookbook
Albertson, 290 pp $5.00
Blue Strawberry Cookbook
J. Haller, 1976, 150 pp $2.50
Blueberry Hill Cookbook
E. Masterson, 1959 .... $17.50
Blueberry Hill Menu Cookbook
E. Masterson, 1963 .... $12.50
Body Building Dishes for Children
1954, pb $4.50
Bon Appetit
Griffith Music, 1951 .... $7.00
Bond Bread Cookbook
1932, 30 pp, pb $5.00
Bond Bread Cookbook
1933, 22 pp, pb $5.00
Bond Bread Cookbook
1935, 73 pp, pb $3.50
Book of Appetizers
H. Brown, 1958, 145 pp $3.00
Book of Better Breakfasts
Postum Cereal, 1925, lf.. $1.25
Book of Breads
Ithica NY, Brewer, 1929, lf $2.00
Book of Cookery
AW, 1591 - 1976 reprint, hb $6.00
Book of Cookies
Bakers Helper, 135 pp $7.50
Book of Cookies
Good Housekeeping, 1958, 68 pp, pb $6.00
Book of Entrees
J. Hill, 1906, hb $18.00

Book of Herb Cookery
   I. Hoffman, 1940, 251 pp **$7.00**
Book of Meals
   Guarracino, 1922, 4th edition **$18.00**
Book of Menus & Recipes
   Lutes, 1936, 213 pp, hb **$10.00**
Book of Savoury Cooking
   M. Pattern, 1961, 594 pp, 1st edition **$7.50**
Borden's Cooking New York World's Fair
   1939, pb **$5.00**
Borden's Eagle Brand Recipes
   1946 .... **$2.00**
Borden's Magic Recipes
   Borden's milk, 1964, lf **$1.00**
Boston Cookbook
   Lincoln, 1899 .... **$45.00**
Boston Cookbook
   Lincoln, 1915 .... **$15.00**

                                                  ᥱᴖ

*Mrs. Lincoln was the first to tabulate ingredients at the
head of a recipe in her first cookbook in 1887.*

                                                  ᥱᴖ

Boston Cooking School Cookbook
   Fannie Farmer, 1906, hb **$60.00**
Boston Cooking School Cookbook
   Fannie Farmer, 1912, 648 pp, hb **$25.00**
Boston Cooking School Cookbook
   Fannie Farmer, 1915, hb **$12.50**
Boston Cooking School Cookbook
   Fannie Farmer, ca. 1920, 656 pp, hb **$25.00**
Boston Cooking School Cookbook
   Fannie Farmer, 1934, 831 pp, hb **$8.00**
Boston Cooking School Cookbook
   Fannie Farmer, 1938, 838 pp, hb **$18.00**
Boston Cooking School Cookbook
   Fannie Farmer, 1942, 830 pp, hb **$13.50**
Boston Cooking School
   Fannie Farmer, 1923, 806 pp, hb **$22.00**
Boston Cooking School
   Fannie Farmer, 1945 .... **$8.50**
Boston Globe Cookbook for Brides
   1950, 118 pp, pb **$5.00**
Boston School Cookbook
   Fannie Farmer, 1927, hb **$10.00**
Boston School Kitchen Test Book
   Lincoln, 1886 .... **$75.00**

The Boston Cooking School Cookbook
Fannie Merritt Farmer
1923

BOUND FOR HOME COOKING

LATTA ROAD
BAPTIST CHURCH

Bound For Home Cooking
Latta Road Baptist Church

Bound for Home Cooking
Latta Road Baptist Church, NY, 83 pp, pb $3.50
Bread & Sandwiches
Good Housekeeping, 1958, 68 pp, pb $2.00
Bread Basket
Fleischmann's, 1945, 40 pp, pb $3.00
Bread, Rolls, Sweet Dough
P. Richards, 1937, 351 pp $10.00
Breads, Biscuits & Rolls - 250 Recipes
Culinary Arts, 1954, pb $4.50
Breakfast for Lovers
L. Lockwood, 1981, pb $4.00
Brer Rabbit Modern Recipes
38 pp $2.50
Brer Rabbit Molasses Recipes
Lf $1.00
Brer Rabbit's Modern Recipes for Modern Living
48 pp, pb $2.25
Brer Rabbit - 94 Goodies
Jordan, 48 pp, pb $3.50
Brer Rabbit - Be Sure To Get Your Iron
Lf $1.00
Bride's Favorite Receipts
Indianapolis, 1909, hb $18.00
Bring Delicacy & Flavor to Daily Cooking
Rumford, 1931, 29 pp $3.00
Brockport's Favorite Recipes
Nativity Church, NY, 1950, pb $6.00
Brown Bag Cookbook
1976, 32 pp $1.50
Brunch Breakfast & Morning Coffee
Cul. Arts, 1955, 68 pp, pb $3.50
Budget Cook Book
Best Foods, 1936 .... $7.00
Buffet Entertaining
Family Cookbook, 1978, hb $2.50
Bull Cook and Authentic Historical Recipes
Herter, 1960, 191 pp, hb, 1st edition $8.50
Burnt Offerings
Christ Church, Florida, 189 pp, pb $5.00
Busy Woman's Cookbook
Williams-Heller, 1951, 342 pp $6.00
Butterick Book of Recipes & Household Helps
1927, 256 pp, hb $18.00
Butterick Cookboo
H. Judson, 1911, 359 pp $9.00
Buttery Shelf Cookbook
T. Tudor $25.00

Breakfast for Lovers
Lu Lockwood

Brer Rabbit Molasses Recipes

Cake and Food Decorating
Wilton, 1956, 16 pp, lf **$2.00**

Cake and Frosting
Betty Crocker, 1966, 144 pp, hb.............................. **$3.00**

Cake Baking Made Easy with Airy Fairy
Cake recipes **$5.00**

Cake Book
Good Housekeeping, 1958, 68 pp, pb **$2.00**

Cake Decorating Cookbook
Cul. Arts, hb **$3.00**

Cake Recipes - 250 Classics
Cul Arts, 1954, pb **$4.50**

Cake Secrets
Ingleheart, 1921.. **$15.00**

Cake Secrets
Iglehearts, purple cover, lf.. **$2.25**

Cakes & Pastries
Carney, 1923 .... **$18.00**

Cakes & Pastries
J. Lambeth, 1937, 351 pp.. **$10.00**

Cakes & Pastries
J. Lambeth, 1938, 115 pp... **$10.00**

Cakes and Cookies with Personality
Best Foods, 1937, 24 pp, lf **$1.25**

Calavo on Your Daily Menu
Avocado Growers, 1934, lf **$2.50**

Calendar of Dinners with 615 Recipes
Story of Crisco, 1921, 231 pp.. **$15.00**

Calendar of Dinners, Story of Crisco
1915, 231 pp **$10.00**

Calendar of Food & Wine
N. Heaton, 270 pp **$5.00**

Calendar Recipes of Dinners
Crisco, 1923, 231 pp, hb **$7.50**

California Fruit Growers . . . Culinary & Toilet
Sunkist, 32 pp, pb **$3.50**

California Prune Surprises
California Cured Fruit, ca. 1900, 48 pp **$2.00**

Calorie Cookbook
M. Donahue, 1923, 250 pp, hb **$6.50**

Calumet Baking Book
1931, 31 pp, pb **$4.50**

Calumet Baking Powder Cookbook
1920, lf.. **$3.50**

Calumet Baking Powder Recipe Book
1922, 80 pp **$12.00**

GOOD HOUSEKEEPING'S

CAKE BOOK

with decorating ideas for many occasions

ONLY 39¢

Good Housekeeping's Cake Book
With Decorating Ideas for Many Occasions

California Fruit Growers Exhange Recipes
Culinary & Toilet
Published by California Fruit Growers Exchange
Los Angeles, California

Calumet Book of Oven Triumphs
1934, 32 pp **$4.50**
Calumet Cookbook
80 pp, 28th edition **$8.50**
Calumet Cookbook
1920, 80 pp, pb **$6.50**
Calumet Cookbook
Kewpie cover **$20.00**
Calumet Reliable Recipes
Boy on cover, 1915 ....**$3.00**
Calumet Reliable Recipes
Boy drumming on cover **$8.00**
Calumet
Figural, 1920's **$6.00**

Campbell's condensed soup was introduced in 1870's.

Campbell Kids Junior
1954 ....**$4.00**
Campbell Soup Can
Figural **$5.00**
Campbell Soup - Easy Ways to Delicious Meals
1967, 203 pp **$6.00**
Campbell's Cooking with a Purpose for Girl Scouts
Ca. 1975, 15 pp, lf **$1.50**
Campfire Marshmallows
1920 ....**$5.00**
Campus Survival Cookbook
J. Wood, 1973, 160 pp, pb **$4.00**
Canalside Cookery
Brockport Symphony Orchestra, 260 pp **$5.00**
Canapé Parade
Scarbough NY, 1932 ....**$3.00**
Candy - 250 Ways to Make
Cul. Arts, 1954, 68 pp, pb **$7.00**
Candy Book
Culinary Arts, R. Berolzheimer, 1941, 48 pp **$4.00**
Candy Book
F. Northcrass, 1958, 48 pp **$3.50**
Candy Cook Book
A. Bradley, 1922, 222 pp **$6.50**
Candy Making at Home
M. Wright, 1920, 188 pp **$20.00**

Captivating Cookery with Allsweet
27 pp, pb $3.00
Carefree Cooking with Frigidaire Electric Range
1940, 48 pp, pb $6.00
Carefree Cooking, Frigidaire Electric Range
1944, 48 pp, lf $3.50
Carillon Cookbook
University of Rochester, NY, 1982, 52 pp, pb $2.00
Carnation Cookbook
M. Blake, 1943, 92 pp $3.00
Carnation's
1939 .... $5.00
Carving & Serving
Lincoln, 1914 .... $25.00
Cash from Your Kitchen
1953, 1984 reprints, 273 pp $4.50
Casserole Book
Good Housekeeping, 1958, 69 pp, pb $4.50
Casserole
Culinary Arts, 1953, pb $4.00
Casseroles
Garden Club Cookbook, 1969, 379 pp, pb $12.00
Catering for Special Occasions
Fannie Farmer, 1911, 229 pp $50.00
Cecil Brownstone's Associated Press Cookbook
1972, 346 pp, pb $8.50
Centaur Almanac
1886 .... $12.00
Central Adirondack Cook Book
American Legion Auxillary, 1934, pb $5.00
Century Cookbook
M. Ronald, 1895 .... $30.00
Ceresota Cookbook
Boy on cover, 1910 .... $2.00
Ceresota Flour Cook
1912 .... $15.00
Certo Insert
General Foods, 1937, 31 pp, lf $1.50
Certo Recipes
1938, lf $2.00
Chafing Dish Possibilites
Fannie Farmer, 1906 .... $18.00
Charity Club
1878 .... $12.50
Charleston Receipts
Junior League, 1950, 330 pp, pb $5.00
Cheap and Nutritious Cookbook
Grey Panthers, San Francisco, 1987, 130 pp $3.50

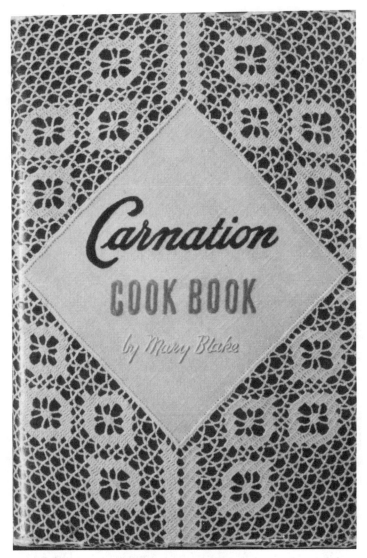

Carnation Cookbook
By Mary Blake

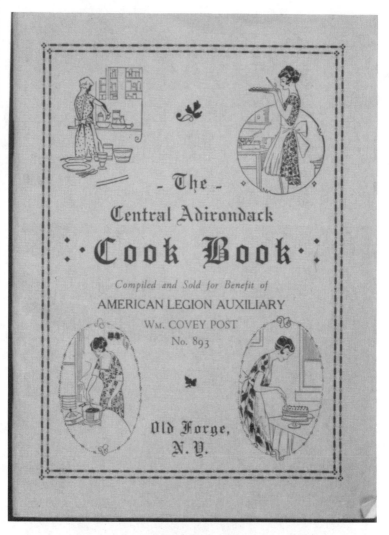

The Central Adirondack Cook Book
Compiled and Sold for Benefit of American Legion Auxiliary
Wm Covey Post No. 893
Old Forge, NY

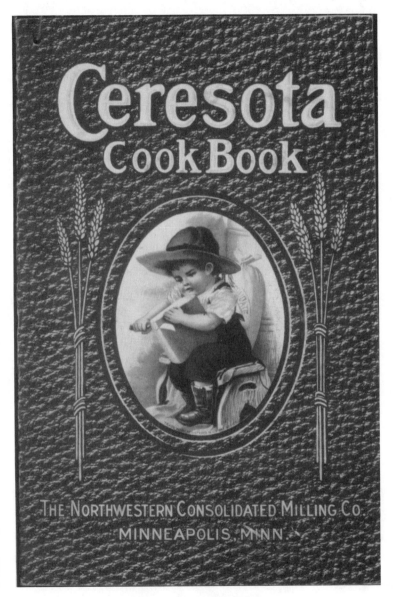

Ceresota Cook Book
The Northwestern Consolidated Milling Co.
Minneapolis, Minn.

Certo Recipes
For Making Perfect Jams, Jellies and Marmalades
"The World's New Standard of Quality"
Copyright 1922 by Pectin Sales Co., Inc.

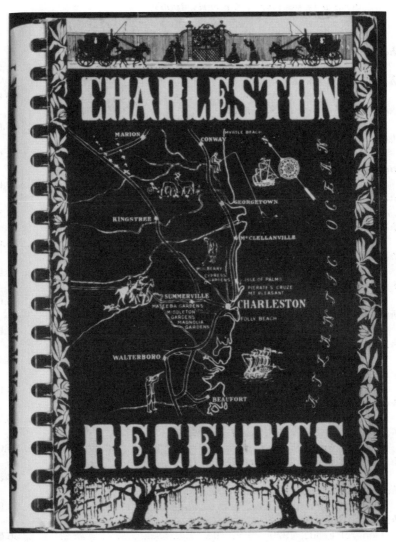

Charleston Receipts
Collected by The Junior League of Charleston
1950

Receipt: a formula or rule for producing something. This term was used until the early 1900's.

Cheap Desserts
H. Peek, 1977, 54 pp $1.25

Cheese & Cheese Cookery
T. Layton, 1972, 242 pp $9.00

Cheese and Ways to Serve It
M. Dahnke, 1931, 46 pp, lf $3.00

Cheese Cookbook
Culinary Arts, 1956 ....$3.00

Chef's Secret Cookbook
Szathemary, 1972, 28 pp $10.00

Chef's Tour
R. Rosen, 1952, 144 pp $3.50

Chemistry of the Household
M. Dodd, 1914, 169 pp, hb $5.00

Cherished Recipes
St. Rocco's Church, NY, 186 pp, pb $4.00

Chicken of the Sea Tuna Hoppy Bar-20 Ranch Recipes
1951 ....$5.00

Children's Party Book
C. Staley, 1935, 23 pp $3.00

Chinese Cookbook
Culinary Arts, 1936, 47 pp, pb $3.00

Chinese Cookery Made Easy
I. Chang, 1959, 256 pp, pb $6.00

Chinese Cooking Secrets
E. Chen, ca. 1960, 177 pp, hb $6.50

Chinese Cooking with American Meals
M. Hodgson, 1970 ....$5.00

Chiquita Banana Presents 18 Recipes
1951, 18 pp, lf $3.50

Chiquita Banana's Recipe Book
1950, 25 pp $2.00

Chocolate Cookery
General Foods, 1929, 36 pp, lf...$6.50

Choice Cookery
F. Owen, 1889 ....$40.00

Choice Recipes Cocoa and Chocolate
Baker's, 1916, 64 pp, pb $9.50

Choice Recipes
Baker's Chocolate, 1914, 64 pp (see page 31) $5.00

Choice Recipes
Miss Parola, 1895, pb $15.00

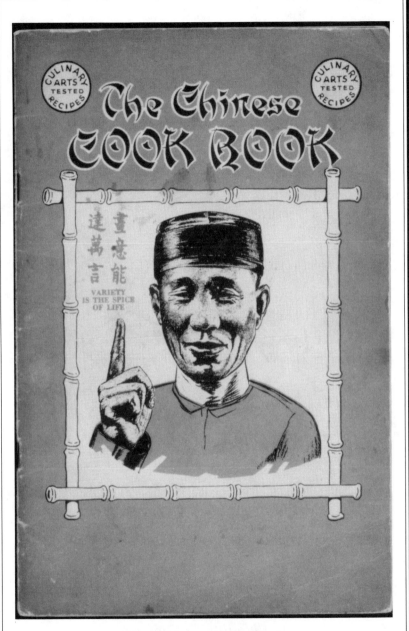

The Chinese Cook Book
By Mr. M. Sing Au
Copyright 1936

CHIQUITA BANANA'S Recipe Book

BANANAS
COOKED, pages 2-7
SALADS 8-13   DESSERTS 14-20, 23
CAKES 16 and 23   COOKIES 17   PIES 18
SAUCES 19   DAIRY DISHES 19-21   BREADS 22-23

*Chiquita Banana's
Recipe Book*

Choice Recipes
W. Baker, 1924, 64 pp, pb $10.00
Choice Recipes for Clever Cooks
L. Allen, 1926, 282 pp $9.00
Choice Recipes of Fish and Seafood
E. Cooley, 1941, 47 pp, pb $3.00
Christmas Crafts & Foods
Woman's Day, 1983, 192 pp, hb $7.00
Christmas-Time Cookbook
Better Homes & Gardens, 1974, 216 pp $10.50
City Wide Flower Club
J. Monteith, 100 pp, pb $3.50
Cookbook Christmas
1935, St. James Guild, MN, 31 pp, pb $6.00
Cookbook Libro de Cocina
Foreign student, SUNY, 1974, 119 pp, pb $5.00
Cooking the Scandinavian Way
Adlerbert, 1961, 267 pp, Czechoslovakia $5.00
Clabber Girl Baking Book
1934, 15 pp $4.00
Clementine in the Kitchen
P. Beck, 1943, 228 pp, hb $7.00
Clementine Paddleford's Cook Young Cookbook
1966, 124 pp, pb $4.00
Cleveland's Superior Receipt
Cleveland Baking Powder, 72 pp, pb $5.00
Co-op Cuisine Cookbook
Brockport Food Coop, 1973, 86 pp $1.50
Cocktail Guide & Ladies Companion
Gaige, 1941, 1st edition $10.00
Cocktails by Jimmy
96 pp, hb $1.00
Coconut Dishes that Everybody Loves
Baker's, 1931, 39 pp, lf $3.00
Coffee Cookery
C. Dryer, HP Books $3.00
Cokesbury Shower Book
K. Fite, 1941, 179 pp, hb $8.00
Colburns Condiment Recipes
24 pp, orange cover $3.00
Coldspot 49 Recipes
15 pp $1.00
Collector Cookbook
1963, 320 pp, pb $3.00
College Woman's Cook Book
1923, 96 pp, 1st edition $10.00
Colonial Cookbook
1911, 287 pp, hb $3.00

Colonial Recipes
M. Bomberger, 1907, 107 pp $8.00
Come Into the Kitchen
D. Jerdon, L. Pinkham, ca. 1920, 32 pp $12.00
Common Sense Cookbook
I. Allen, 1939, 117 pp $6.00
Common Sense Papers on Cookery
Payne, ca. 1920 .... $30.00
Company Meals & Buffets
Good Housekeeping, 1958, 68 pp, pb $2.00
Compendium of Cooking & Knowledge
1890 .... $15.00
Complete Bean Cookbook
V. Bennett, 1969, 298 pp $8.00
Complete Blueberry Cookbook
E. Barton, 1974, 156 pp, hb $6.00
Complete Book of Etiquette
Rivers, 1934, 514 pp $4.00
Complete Book of Outdoor Cookery
J. Beard, 1955, 255 pp, hb $6.50
Complete Book of Table Setting
A. Hill, 1949 .... $4.50
Complete Family Cookbook
Curtain products, 1970, 444 pp, hb $6.00
Complete Gourmet Cooking in the American Kitchen
M. Waldo, 1960, 374 pp $3.00
Complete Hostess
A. Zinkeisen, 1936, hb $15.00
Complete Oriental Cooking
M. Waldo, 1962, 246 pp $2.00
Complete Pie Cookbook
Farm Journal, Nichols, 1965, 308 pp, hb $2.50
Complete Potatoe Cookbook
R. Bakalar, 1969, 312 pp $2.50
Complete Recipe Book
1929, 47 pp, lf $9.00
Complete Round the World Meat Cookbook
M. Waldo, 1967, 492 pp, hb $9.00
Complete Vegetable Cookery
M. Waldo, 1962, 186 pp $2.00
Concordia Cooks
Lutheran Church, Kendall, NY, 1982, 50 pp, pb $3.00
Confessions of a Sneaky Cook
Kinderlehrer, 1971, 245 pp $8.00
Congress Cookbook
Congress Yeast Powder, 1899, 80 pp, pb $5.00
Congressional Club Cookbook
1927 .... $18.00

Connecticut Cookbook
Women's Club Westport, 1944, 261 pp, hb **$15.00**
Consolidated Library of Modern Cook & Household Recipes
1904, 346 pp, hb **$5.00**
Continental Cookbook
J. Bonne, 1928, 386 pp **$12.00**
Continental Cookery
1963, 50 pp, hb **$1.50**
Continental Cookery for the English Table
Siepen, 1915, 1st edition **$22.50**
Continental Cuisine Classics
G. Musser, Volume I, 90 pp, pb **$2.00**
Control Your Weight With Knox Gelatin
1938, 22 pp, pb **$1.50**
Convalescent's Recipe Book
G. Osgood, 1901, 162 pp **$13.00**
Convection Oven Cookbook
Reynolds, 1980 .... **$2.00**
Cookbook
1940, Spencerport, NY, pb **$4.00**
Cookbook
J. Roth, 96 pp, pb **$1.00**
Cookbook
W. Moody, 1931, 475 pp **$12.50**
Cook Book & Business Directory
Sister Society; Rochester, NY, 1939, 40 pp, pb **$6.00**
Cook Book for All Occasions
DeBoth, 1936, 192 pp, hb **$8.00**
Cook Book
Kendall Home Bureau, NY, 1929, 85 pp, pb **$4.00**
Cook It In A Casserole
M. Barrows, 1943, 183 pp, hb **$8.00**
Cook Not Mad or Rational Cookery
Watertown, 1831 .... **$200.00**
Cook Tour with Minute Tapioca
1931, 46 pp, pb **$4.00**
Cook with Love
Amaretto di Saronno, 1976, 31 pp, pb **$1.00**
Cook's Oracle
M. Francis, 1822 .... **$95.00**
Cookbook for Men
L. Lehr, 1949, 208 pp, hb **$6.50**
Cookbook for Two
Ida Allen, 1957, 320 pp **$5.00**
Cookbook for Ulcer Patients
W. Aurell, 1950, 100 pp, hp **$4.00**
Cookbook Historic Rochester, NY
Sesq., 47 pp, pb **$6.50**

Cook Book

AND

BUSINESS DIRECTORY

Salem Evangelical and Reformed Church, Rochester, N. Y.

Published by

THE SISTER SOCIETY

— of —

Salem Evangelical and Reformed Church
ROCHESTER, N. Y.

Cook Book and Business Directory
Published by The Sister Society
Salem Evangelical and Reformed Church
Rochester, NY

Cook with Love
Amaretto di Saronno

Cookbook of Leftover
H. Clarke, 1911, 263 pp, hb.. $15.00
Cookbook of Useful Household Hints
F. Owens, 1883 .... $25.00
Cookbook Women's Association
LFP Church, Washington, 53 pp, pb $3.50
Cookbook Women's Day
1958, 96 pp, pb $3.50
Cookery Calendar 1925
Women World Magazine, 56 pp, hb $16.00
Cookery for Today
Delineator Magazine, 1932, 164 pp, hb $5.00
Cookery Notebook
Mechanics Inst., lf.. $5.00
Cookie Book
Culinary Arts, 1939, 48 pp, pb $6.00
Cookie Book
Watts, 1937 .... $5.00
Cookie Cookbook
D. Clem, 1966, 2nd edition.. $7.50
Cookie-Craft
Parkay, lf.. $1.00
Cooking Afloat
Pinkerton, 1959, 279 pp $6.50
Cooking Bold and Fearless for Men
Sunset, 1969, 160 pp, pb $3.00
Cooking by the Calendar
Family Weekly, Hensen, 1978, 308 pp, hb $4.00
Cooking by the Garden Calendar
Mattson, 1st edition, signed $3.00
Cooking Calendar
Betty Crocker, 1962, 176 pp, hb.................................. $1.50
Cooking Favorites of Spencerport NY Fire Department
40 pp, pb $3.00
Cooking for Company
Farm Journal, 1968, 412 pp.. $10.00
Cooking for Crowds
1927, 19 pp, lf.. $3.50
Cooking for Many
C. Turgeon, 1962, hb $4.00
Cooking For One
B. Parker, 1955, 122 pp, hb.. $5.00
Cooking For One
RG & E NY, 27 pp, pb $2.00
Cooking For A Crowd
Better Homes & Garden, 1929, 53 pp, pb $3.00
Cooking for Two
J. Hill, 1906, pb $20.00

Cooking for Two
J. Hill, 1931, 362 pp, hb $9.00
Cooking Hints and Tested Recipes
W. Carter, 1937, 32 pp, pb $3.00
Cooking Holiday Inn Way
R. Malone, 1962, 209 pp, pb $4.00
Cooking in Clay
I. Chalmer, 1974, 45 pp, pb $3.00
Cooking in the Nude - For Playful Gourmets
1987, 64 pp, pb $3.00
Cooking in the Nude - For Red Hot Lovers
1987, 64 pp, pb $3.00
Cooking Menu Service
I. Allen, 1934-35 .... $5.50
Cooking of India
Time-Life, 1969 .... $5.00
Cooking School of the Air
General Foods, 1932 and 1934, 100 pp $8.00
Cooking the Cape Cod Way
Heritage Shop, ca. 1940, 16 pp, lf $5.00
Cooking the Chinese Way
Fround, 1962, 224 pp $2.00
Cooking the Greek Way
M. Duncan, 1964, 256 pp, hb $5.00
Cooking the Jewish Way
Wall, 1961, 207 pp, hb $2.00
Cooking the Modern Ways
Planters Oil, 1948, 39 pp, lf $2.50
Cooking with a French Touch
G. Maurois, 1951, 239 pp $8.00
Cooking with a Velvet Touch
Carnation, ca. 1960, 48 pp, lf $4.00
Cooking with Condensed Soups
A. Marshall, Campbell's, 48 pp $2.00
Cooking with Curry
F. Brobeck, 1952, 192 pp $6.00
Cooking with Sour Cream and Buttermilk
Culinary Arts, 1955, 68 pp, pb $3.00
Cooking with Steamers
1981, 48 pp, pb $1.00
Cooking with Susan
G. House, 1967, 64 pp... $1.50
Cookology
San-i-fla, 48 pp, pb $4.00
Cook's Book
KC Baking Powder, 1933 .... $3.00
Cook's Digest
Nov. 1940, 70 pp, lf.. $2.00

Cook's Handbook
  Leith, 1981 .... **$7.50**
Cook's Oracle & Housekeeper's Manual
  W. Kitchener, 1830 .... **$100.00**
Cook's Tour with Minute Tapioca
  1931, 46 pp, lf **$2.50**
Cooling Dishes for Hot Weather
  Culinary Arts, 1956, 56 pp, pb **$3.00**
Copco Pots & Pans Cookbook
  Seranne, 276 pp **$7.50**
Copper Kettle Cook Book
  M. Dixon, 1963, 480 pp **$7.50**
Cordon Bleu Cookbook
  D. Lucas, 1951, 322 pp, hb **$6.00**
Corned Beef & Caviar
  Hillis, 1937, 196 pp **$7.00**
Cornell Bulletin for Homemaker
  Canning, June 1933, 74 pp, pb **$5.00**
Correct Salads for All Occasions
  Hellmann's, 1931, 30 pp, lf **$3.00**
Cosmopolitan Cookery
  L. Deeley, 1945, 167 pp **$6.00**
Cottolene Recipes
  1893, lf **$3.00**
Cottolene Shortening
  1905 .... **$10.00**
Cottolene Shortening - 52 Sunday Dinners
  1915, 192 pp **$4.00**
Country Art of Blueberry Cookery
  C. Morrison, 1972, 119 pp **$4.00**
Country Cookbook
  D. Brown, 1937, 221 pp **$5.00**
Country Flavor
  Pearson, 1962 .... **$7.00**
Country Food
  M. Ungerer, 1983, 247 pp **$9.00**
Country Kitchen
  D. Lutes, 1937, 261 pp, hb **$12.00**
Country Kitchen Cook Book
  E. Meath, 1968, 238 pp **$7.50**
Cow Brand Cookbook
  1900, 32 pp, lf **$3.00**
Cow Brand Soda
  1934 .... **$2.50**
Cox's Delicious Recipes
  Cox Gelatin, 1933, 30 pp, lf **$2.25**
Cox's Manual of Gelatin Cookery
  Scotland, 1914, 64 pp, pb **$4.50**

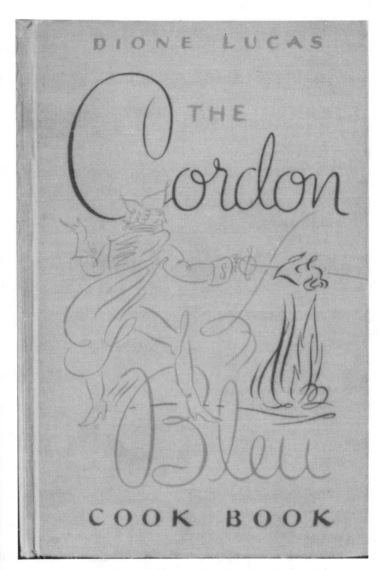

The Cordon Bleu Cook Book
by Dione Lucas

Cozinah Bahiana
    D. Brandao, Spanish, 1948, 71 pp, pb **$3.00**
Cream of Wheat
    Diamond Cookbook, 1910 .... **$20.00**
Creative Cooking Made Easy
    Golden Fluffo, 1956, 108 pp **$3.00**
Creative Table Settings
    Better Homes & Gardens, 1972, 96 pp, hb **$2.50**
Creole Cookbook
    Culinary Arts, 1956, 68 pp, pb **$3.00**
Creole Cookbook
    Picayune, 1971, hb **$6.00**
Crepe Cookery
    M. Hoffman, 1976, 176 pp **$3.50**
Cricket Tea Room Cookbook
    T. Perry, 1940 .... **$3.50**
Crisco
    1916 .... **$5.00**
Crockery Cookery
    M. Hoffman, 1975, 176 pp, pb **$4.50**
Cross Creek Cookery
    Rawlings, 1942 .... **$27.50**
Crown Cork & Seal Canning Book
    1936, pb **$5.00**
Cucumbers, Melons and Squash
    Natl Gardener, 1987, 87 pp **$5.00**
Culinary American
    E. Brown, 1961, 1st edition **$30.00**
Culinary Capers
    Evanston, Ill., 1941, 527 pp **$5.00**
Culinary Classics & Improvisations
    Field, 1967, 223 pp **$10.00**
Culinary Crafting
    D. Townsend, 1976, 192 pp, hb **$3.00**
Culinary Gems . . . Of Choice Recipes
    J. Cadle, Mass., 1884 .... **$16.00**
Cupid's Cookbook
    1933, hb **$15.00**
Cut Up Cakes
    Baker's Coconut, 1956, lf **$2.00**
Cutco Cookbook
    Cutco Cutlery, 1956, 128 pp **$5.00**
Czechoslovakia Pastries
    1957, 106 pp **$4.00**

D-Zerta
1930, 32 pp $9.00
Dagmar Freuchen's Cookbook of the Seven Seas
1968, 256 pp, hb $8.00
Daily Cookery from Breakfast to Supper
Sproat, 1923 .... $10.00
Daily News Cook Book
J. Eddington, 1925, 64 pp $4.00
Dainty Desserts for Dainty People
Knox Gelatine, 1924, 41 pp, lf....................................... $5.00
Dainty Dishes from Foreign Lands
L. Rice, 1911 .... $20.00
Dairy 300 Healthful Dishes
1954, pb $4.50
Dairy Cookbook
R. Berolzheimer, 1941 .... $5.00
Dances & Cooking Specialties of Spain
Women's Club Madrid, 1965, 110 pp, pb $5.00
DAR Cookbook
1949, 366 pp, pb $6.50
Daughter-in-law Cookbook
H. Burrnett, 1969, 318 pp $10.00
Davis Cookbook
Davis Baking Powder, 1904, 62 pp, pb $6.00
Deep Sea Recipes
Gorton-Pew, ca. 1930, lf.. $2.50
Delectable Desserts
Culinary Arts, 1940, 48 pp, pb....................................... $4.00
Delectable Desserts
Good Housekeeping, 1958, 68 pp, pb $2.00
Delicious New Combinations of Inexpensive Favorites
Pet Milk, 31 pp, lf... $1.00
Delicious Desserts
HP Books, 1985, 130 pp $3.50
Delicious Diet Cookbook
L. Lavine, 1974, 150 pp $1.00
Delicious Lamb Dishes
National Livestock Association, 1935 .... $2.00
Delicious Quick Desserts
Junket, 1929, 24 pp, lf.. $3.00
Delightful Cooking With Three Pro Corn
Indian Child, pb $5.00
Delineator Cookbook
Delineator Home Institute, 1928, 788 pp, hb $30.00
Delineator Home Institute - New Delineator Recipes
1930, 222 pp $6.00

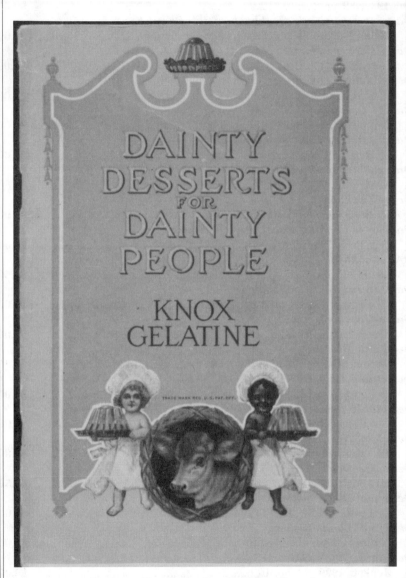

Dainty Desserts for Dainty People
Knox Gelatine

Delmonte Fruit Book
1924, 32 pp, pb $3.00
Dennison Party Book for Children & Teens
1958 .... $1.25
Dessert 250 Delectable
Culinary Arts, 1954, pb $4.50
Dessert Book
Boston, 1872 .... $12.50
Dessert Cookbook
Southern Living, 1971, hb $2.00
Desserts of the World
Jell-o $5.00
Desserts, Garden Club Cookbook
Ca. 1960, 382 pp, pb $12.00
Desserts
Hulse, 1912, 154 pp, hb $12.00
Detroit Jewel Store
32 pp $9.00
Devine Desserts
B. Hurst, 1986, 128 pp, hb $3.00
Dictionary of Foods
1932, 135 pp $5.00
Dictionary of Gastronomy
Simon & Hobert, 1970, 397 pp $15.00
Diet for a Small Planet
F. Lappe, 410 pp, pb $3.00
Dinah Shore Cook Book
1973, 386 pp $6.00
Diner's Club Cookbook
M. Waldo, 1959, 241 pp $6.00
Dining Car Cookbook & Serving Instructions
Union Pacific Railroad $28.00
Dining Car Recipes
1952, calendar $4.00
Dining Delights - French
1948, 30 pp $3.50
Dining in the Great Cruise Ships
J. DeMers, 1987, 200 pp $3.00
Dinner at Omar Khyyam's
G. Mardikian, 1944, 150 pp, hb, signed $12.00
Dione Lucas Meat & Poultry Cookbook
1955, 324 pp $7.00
Discover Gold
Galliano, 1972, 24 pp, lf $1.00
Dishes for All Year Round
S. Rorer, 1903, 62 pp, lf $6.00
Dishes for Special Occasions
E. Blair, 1975, 312 pp, hb $2.50

Dishes Men Like
Worcestershire, 1952, 63 pp **$2.50**
Dishes of Fishes
L. Salmon, 1962, 15 pp, pb **$1.50**
Dispenser Soda Water Guide
Haynes, 1909 .... **$8.00**
Doctor's Quick Inches Off Diet
Stillman, 1969, 311 pp **$5.00**
Domestic Receipt Book
Beecher, 1855 .... **$85.00**
Domestic Science Recipes for Elementary School
Rochester, NY, 1924, 83 pp, pb **$5.00**
Donon Club Cookbook
Donon Club, 1927, 209 pp **$10.00**
Dorchester Woman's Club Cookbook
Boston, ca. 1900, 146 pp **$30.00**
Doubleday Cookbook, Volume I
J. Anderson, 1975, 780 pp **$3.50**
Down on the Farm Cookbook
H. Worth, 1943, 322 pp **$13.00**
Down Right Delicious Sunmaid Raisin Recipes
Heinz, 32 pp, lf **$1.00**
Dr. A.W. Chase Candy Book
32 pp **$3.00**
Dr. Caldwell Home Cookbook
Pepsin Syrup, ca. 1910, 32 pp **$3.00**
Dr. Chase's Recipes or Information for Everybody
1880, 400 pp **$25.00**
Dr. Chase's Recipes
A. Chase, 1866, 384 pp, hb, reprint **$8.00**
Dr. Morse's Indian Root Pills Cookbook
1896, 32 pp **$7.00**
Dr. Pierce's Good Cooking
Ca. 1900, 32 pp, pb **$3.00**
Dr. Price's Baking Powder
1915 .... **$8.00**
Drink Dole's Pineapple
1906, lf **$3.00**
Dry It - You'll Like It!
G. MacManiman, 1974, 74 pp, pb **$4.00**
Duncan Hines Food Odyssey
1955, 274 pp, hb **$6.00**
Dundee President Cookbook
Women's Auxillary, 1930, 256 pp **$12.00**
Durkie Famous Food Cookbook
Century of Progress, 1933 .... **$5.00**

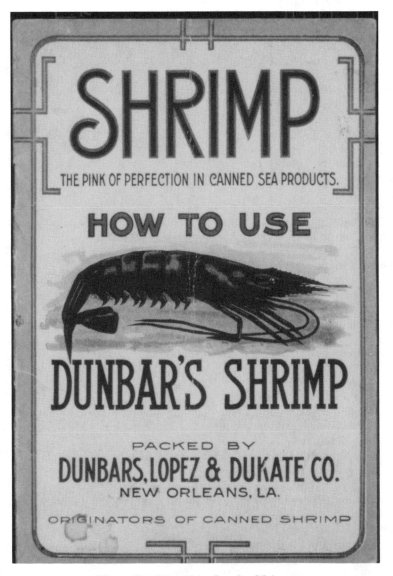

How To Use Dunbar's Shimp
Packed by Dunbars, Lopex & Dukate Co.
New Orleans, LA

Eagle Brand Recipes
56 pp, pb **$4.00**
Easier Cooking for 2, 4 or 6
M. Taylor, Pet Milk, 15 pp **$3.00**
East - West Book of Rice Cookry
M. Tracy, 1952 ....**$4.00**
Easy Entertaining
C. Benton, 1917, 257 pp **$6.00**
Easy Gourmet's Dishes
C. Adams, 72 pp, pb **$1.00**
Easy Preserving for Victory
1943, 36 pp w/labels, pb **$3.00**
Easy Steps in Cooking
J. Fryer, 1913 ....**$35.00**
Easy to Make Pickles and Relishes
L. Dudgeon, Cornell, 11 pp, lf **$2.00**
Eat, Drink & Be Merry in Maryland
Steiff, 1932 ....**$27.50**
Eat Well on a Dollar a Day
B. Kasing, 1976, pb **$2.00**
Eating in Bed Cookbook
Byfield, 1962, 132 pp, hb...**$8.00**
Economical Cookbook, Arlington Edition
J. Warren, ca. 1890, 96 pp...**$5.00**
Economical Cook Book - All-Round Cookery & Hints
C. Doring, 1929 ....**$15.00**
Economical Cookbook
S. Paul, 1907, 338 pp...**$8.50**
Economy in Food
M. Wellman, 1918, 36 pp, hb **$5.00**
Economy Recipes
Blue Bonnet Margarine, 1939, lf **$1.50**
Edna Eby Heller's Dutch Cookbook
1953, 64 pp, pb **$5.00**
Edwardian Glamour Cooking Without Tears
E. Hugh, 1960, 61 pp, hb **$7.00**
Egg-free, Milk-Free, Wheat-Free
274 pp, 1982 ....**$4.00**
Eggs & Cheese, Spaghetti & Rice
Good Housekeeping, 1958, 68 pp, pb..............................**$2.00**
Eggs - 300 Ways to Serve
Culinary Arts, 1954, pb **$4.50**
Eggs I Have Known
Griffith, 1955, 230 pp, hb **$4.00**
Eggs Summer-Side Up
American Egg Board, 1973, 31 pp, lf **$2.00**

Easy Preserving For Victory
Compiled by Demetria M. Taylor

Edna Eby Heller's Dutch Cookbook
First Edition - 1953
Revised - 1960

Eggs - Facts & Fancies
A. Barrows, 1890 .... **$25.00**
El Molino Cookbook
1976, 144 pp, pb **$7.00**
Elam's Recipe Book
Elam's Whole Grain, 31 pp, lf **$2.50**
Electric Cooking with Your Kenmore
1941 .... **$2.00**
Electric Refrigerator Menus
General Electric, 1927, 144 pp, hb **$18.00**
Elegant Desserts
Culinary Arts, 1955, 68 pp, pb **$3.00**
Elsie the Cow
Botsford, NY, 1952 .... **$15.00**
Elsie's Cookbook
Borden's, 374 pp, hb **$9.00**
Elsie's Star Recipes
Borden's, ca. 1950's, lf **$1.50**
Enchanted Broccoli Forest
M. Katzen, 1982, 307 pp, pb **$8.00**
Encyclopedia of Cooking
M. Ginesn, 1947, 847 pp **$15.00**
Encyclopedia of Fruits, Vegetables, Nuts and Seeds
J. Kadans, 1973, 214 pp, hb **$6.50**
Encyclopedia of Cooking & Homemaking
R. Berolzheimer, 1939, 815 pp, hb **$10.00**
Encyclopedia of Cooking & Homemaking
Culinary Arts, 1940, set of 20 .... **$20.00**
Encyclopedia of European Cooking
M. Soper, 1962, 631 pp, hb **$8.00**
Encyclopedia of Cookery
W. Wise, 1948, 1,269 pp, hb **$22.00**
Encyclopedia of Gastronomy
Simon, 1952, 1st edition **$15.00**
Encyclopedia of Practical Cookery
T. Garrett, ca. 1890, hb **$180.00**
Enterprise Co. Cookbook
1906 .... **$20.00**
Enterprising Housekeeper Recipe Book
1902, 90 pp **$15.00**
Enterprising Housekeeper
Johnson, 1898, 79 pp, pb **$25.00**
Enterprising Housekeeper
1906 .... **$10.00**
Enterprising Housekeeper
1913 .... **$8.00**
Entertaining with Elegance
G. Darioux, 1965, 404 pp **$7.00**

Entertaining with Elizabeth Craig
1933, 312 pp $20.00
Entertaining with Insects
R. Taylor, 1976, 159 pp, pb $6.00
Epicure & Charcoal
A. Simms, 1955, 104 pp $6.00
Escoffier Cookbook
A. Escoffier, 1941, 883 pp $10.00
Esquire Cook Book
1956, 322 pp $7.50
Esquire Party Cookbook
1965, 314 pp $8.00
Esquire Handbook for Hosts
1953, 288 pp, hb $12.00
European Desserts for American Kitchens
1962, 242 pp, hb $5.00
Every Good Cook Knows Another Good Cook
Splint, 1930, 252 pp $10.00
Everyday Cookbook & Family Compendium
316 pp $15.00
Everyday Cookbook
1892 .... $20.00
Everyday Cookbook
Daw's 1937, 157 pp, pb $3.00
Everyday Recipes
Wesson Oil, 1929, 46 pp, pb $4.00
Everyday Recipes
Wesson Oil, 1932 .... $8.00
Everything for the Rice Table
Conimex, 1960, 33 pp $2.00
Excellent Recipes for Baking
Fleischmann Yeast, 1912, 56 pp $2.50
Exotic Fruit Cookbook
Henderson, 1970, 32 pp, pb $2.00
Experimental Cookery
Lowe, 1937 .... $4.00

Fabulous Eggs Book
 J. Feinman, 127 pp, pb **$2.00**
Fairy Tale Cookbook
 C. MacGregory, 1982, 86 pp, hb **$5.00**
Falls Is Cooking
 Niagara Falls, 1985, 94 pp **$3.00**
Family Circle Dessert Cookbook
 1978, hb **$2.50**
Family Circle Fish and Poultry
 1955, 144 pp, hb **$3.50**
Family Cookbook in Color
 M. Pattern, 1973, 349 pp **$1.00**
Family Food Supply
 Metro Life, 1934 .... **$5.00**
Family Tradition
 Magic Baking Powder, 32 pp **$2.50**
Famous Dishes from Every State
 Frigidaire, 1936, pb **$2.00**
Famous New Orleans Drinks
 Arthur, 1938, 96 pp **$3.00**
Famous Personality of Flight Cookbook
 M. Henderson, 1981, 136 pp, pb **$3.00**
Famous Sportsman's Recipes
 DeBoth, 1940, 95 pp **$12.00**
Fan Fare - Rochester NY Philharmonic Orchestra
 1981, 312 pp **$4.50**

∽

Fannie Farmer's Boston Cookbook was first published in 1896.

∽

Fannie Farmer Boston Cooking School Cookbook
 1897 .... **$75.00**
Fannie Farmer Cookbook
 1906 .... **$18.00**
Fannie Farmer Cookbook
 1920 .... **$17.00**
Fannie Farmer Cookbook
 1965, 554 pp **$12.00**
Fannie Farmer Cookbook
 1968, 648 pp, pb **$4.00**
Fannie Farmer Junior Cookbook
 Perkins, 1942, 208 pp, hb **$6.00**
Farm House Cooking
 Pugh, local, 22 pp **$2.50**

Farm Journal
1959, 420 pp **$10.00**
Farmer's Almanac Cookbook
1965, 390 pp, pb **$3.00**
Farmer's Pride Recipe Book
31 pp **$3.50**
Fascinating Cranberries and How to Serve
1937, lf **$3.00**
Fast & Fancy Cookery
J. Cranwell, 1959, 239 pp, hb.. **$5.00**
Favorite Recipes of Wellesley Alumnae
75th Anniversary, 144 pp, pb **$10.00**
Favorite Apple Recipes
G. Foster, Cornell, 16 pp **$1.00**
Favorite Dartmouth Recipes
Field, 220 pp, pb **$4.00**
Favorite Recipes from Marye Danhke's File
Kraft, 1938 .... **$2.00**
Favorite Recipes, Hamlin United Methodist Church, NY
1987, 78 pp **$1.50**
Favorite Recipes of Famous Women
F. Stratton, 1925, 119 pp **$12.00**
Favorite Recipes of Presbyterian Women - Desserts
1968, 382 pp, pb **$6.50**
Favorite Recipes
Center Church, Manchester, Conn., 1954, 187 pp, pb **$5.00**
Favorite Recipes
L. Pinkham, ca. 1930, 32 pp... **$3.50**
Favorite Recipes from the United Nations
1956, pb **$5.00**
Favorite Torte and Cake Recipes
Harbaugh, 1951, 163 pp.. **$4.00**
Feasts Made Fast with R&R Chicken
Ca. 1940, 27 pp **$2.50**
Feed Me! I'm Yours
V. Lansky, 1974, pb... **$2.00**
Feeding the Child from Crib to College
Wheatena, 1928, 44 pp **$12.50**
Fengold Cookbook for Hyperactive Children
1979, 327 pp, pb **$2.50**
Festive Touch
Pet Milk, 1961 .... **$1.50**
Few Cooking Suggestions
Crisco, 1927 .... **$4.00**
Ficher's Blend Baking Book
1941, 164 pp, pb **$4.00**
Fifty Years and Still Cooking
Hemlock Twig, NY, 1977 .... **$4.00**

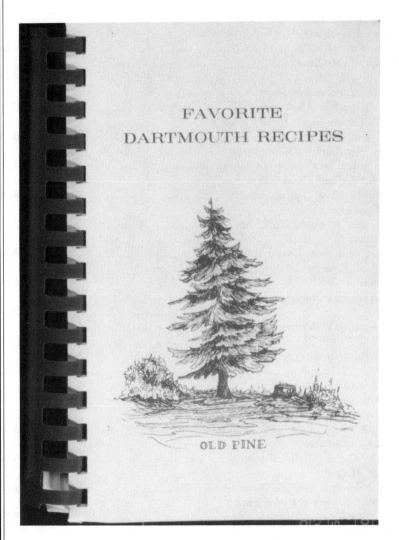

Favorite Dartmouth Recipes

Fine Old Dixie Recipes
 1939 ....$15.00
Finer Fruits
 31 pp, pb $2.00
Fire-King Casserole Recipes
 1944 ....$6.00
Fireless Cookbook
 M. Mitchell, 1911, 315 pp $10.00
Fireside Cook Book
 J. Beard, 1949, 322 pp...$20.00
First Ladies Cookbook
 M. Klapthor, 1969 ....$9.00
Fish & Game Cook Book
 H. Botsford, 1947 ....$10.00
Fish & Seafood - 250 Recipes
 Culinary Arts, 1954, 48 pp, pb $4.50
Fish & Seafood Cook Book
 Brown, 1940, 349 pp, hb $9.00
Fish Cookery
 Spencer & Cobb, 1921, 348 pp $12.00
Flag Brand
 Fort Stanwick, Conn, 1925, 35 pp $5.50
Flavor of France
 Hasting, 1964, 232 pp $20.00
Fleischmann's Recipes
 1906 ....$3.00
Fleischmann's Recipes
 1910, 26 pp, pb $30.00
Fleischmann's Recipes
 1917, 47 pp, pb $4.00
Fleischmann's Recipes
 1924, 48 pp, lf...$2.50
Florida Oranges & Grapefruit for Health
 1929, 31 pp $5.50
Fondue Cookbook
 E. Callahan, 1968, 104 pp $4.00
Fondue Magic
 A. Prichard, 1969, 192 pp, hb..$1.50
Food & Cookery for the Sick
 Fannie Farmer, 1906, 300 pp $28.00
Food and Diet
 J. Pereira, 1870, 322 pp $17.50
Food Conspiracy Cookbook
 L. Wickstrom, 1974, 144 pp, hb $3.00
Food Delights - Macaroni, Spaghetti, Noodles
 1922 ....$2.50
Food Economy Recipes for Leftovers
 Knox, 35 pp $1.00

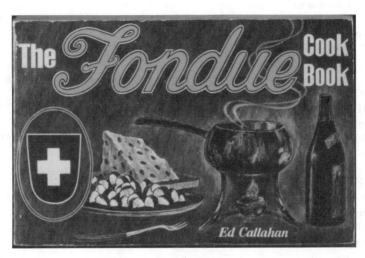

The Fondue Cookbook
Ed Callahan

Food Economy
    Knox, blue triangle cover **$2.50**
Food Favorites
    Kraft, 1951, 32 pp, pb **$1.50**
Food Flashes
    G. Chase, 1947, 71 pp **$3.00**
Food For Goodness Sake
    Meyer, 1973, 176 pp, hb **$1.50**
Food from Sunny Lands
    Dromedary, 1925, pb **$5.00**
Food Triumphs with New Minute Tapioca
    General Foods, 1934, 47 pp, lf **$4.00**
Foodarama Party Book
    Kelvinator, 1959, 128 pp **$3.00**
For Luncheon & Supper Guests
    A. Bradley, 1923, 96 pp **$7.00**
For Making Good Things To Eat
    Wesson Oil, 1932, 46 pp, lf **$3.00**
For Men Only Cookbook
    Abdullah, 1937, 205 pp, hb **$9.00**
For The Hostess
    Kelvinator, 21 pp, pb **$4.50**

Ford Times Cookbook
  Kennedy, 1968, 253 pp, hb $18.00
Formal Dinners
  J. Gooding, 1940, 188 pp $8.00
Forum Feast
  NJ, 1968, 300 pp, pb $4.00
Four Seasons Cookbook
  C. Adams, 1971, 319 pp, hb $12.00
Four Seasons Salads Creative Cuisine
  HP Books, 1985, 80 pp $2.00
Frances Parkinson Keys Cookbook
  1955 .... $24.00
Frankly Fancy Foods
  Betty Crocker, 1959, 26 pp, pb $2.00
French Chef Cookbook
  J. Child, 1968, 440 pp $15.00
French Cook
  Ude, 1978 .... $7.50
French Cooking for All
  Voison, ca. 1920 .... $12.00
French Dressings for Your Favorite Salads
  Kraft, 1957, 22 pp, lf $2.00
French Home Cooking
  dePratz, 1956, 308 pp $5.00
French Household Cooking
  Keyzer, 1928 .... $15.00
French Provincial Cooking
  E. David, 1962, 504 pp, hb, 1st edition $7.00
French's Mustard Junior Cookbook
  1921 .... $6.00
Fresh-kept
  A. Price $3.50
Frigidaire Recipes
  1929, 91 pp $6.00
Frigidaire Recipes
  1939, 36 pp $2.50
Frigidaire
  1926, 16 pp $5.00
From Garden to Kitchen
  Middleton, 1937, 1st edition $15.00
From Hearth to Cookstove - Collectibles of Kitchens
  Franklin, 1976 .... $15.50
From Jamaica to Tables of World
  Canada Dry, 1928, 32 pp, pb $4.00
From My Kitchen to Yours
  C. King, councilwoman, 24 pp, 1963, pb $2.00
From Our Kitchen
  Adoptive Mothers Auxiliary, NJ, 1974, 60 pp, pb $3.00

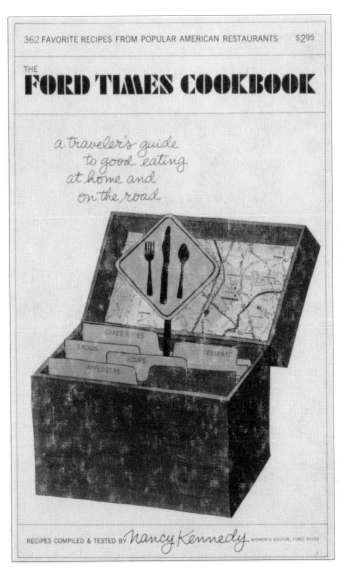

362 FAVORITE RECIPES FROM POPULAR AMERICAN RESTAURANTS $2⁹⁵

THE
FORD TIMES COOKBOOK

*a traveler's guide
to good eating
at home and
on the road*

CAKES & PIES

SALADS

SOUPS

DESSERTS

APPETIZERS

RECIPES COMPILED & TESTED BY *Nancy Kennedy* WOMEN'S EDITOR, FORD TIMES

The Ford Times Cookbook
**Recipes compiled and tested by Nancy Kennedy,
Women's Editor, Ford Times**

FROM OUR KITCHEN

ADOPTIVE MOTHERS AUXILIARY

Childrens Aid and Adoption Society

of New Jersey

From Our Kitchen
Adoptive Mother's Auxiliary
Children's Aid and Adoption Society of New Jersey

From Soup to Pie
Merrell-Soule, ca. 1900, lf $2.00
From the Tripocia to Your Table
Fruit Disp., 1926, lf $3.50
Fruit & Flower Mission Cookbook
1924, 393 pp $10.50
Fruit and Their Cookery
H. Nelson, 1921 .... $18.00
Fun Filled Butter Cookies
Pillsbury, 49 pp, lf $3.00
Fun To Cook Book
Blake, 1955 .... $3.00
Fun With Cooking
M. Freeman, 1947, 58 pp $9.00
Fun With Your Ice Cream Freezer
Electric Co., 16 pp $2.00

Galley Guide
A. Moffat, 1923, 129 pp **$9.00**
Galloping Gourmet
G. Kerr, 1962, 118 pp **$4.00**
Galloping Gourmet
G. Kerr, 1975, 284 pp, hb **$8.00**
Game Cookery
Esturdivant, 1969, 166 pp, hb **$4.50**
Garden Club Cookbook Salads
Mont. Fed. Garden, 1970, 382 pp, pb **$7.00**
Garden Club Meats
1968, 392 pp, pb **$8.00**
Gardeners and Gourmets
Floating Bridge Gardeners, Wash., 1964, pb **$3.50**
Gardeners in the Kitchen
Castle, Rochester, NY, 1969, pb **$1.00**
Gastronomical Me
Pearce, 1943 .... **$25.00**
Gastronomique: a Cookbook for Gourmets
1958, 384 pp **$10.00**
Gem Chopper Cookbook
Sargent & Co., 1902, hb **$9.00**
General Federations of Women's Clubs
CB, Seranne, 1967, 796 pp **$12.50**
General Food Cookbook
General Foods, 1967 pp, hb **$7.50**
General Foods Cookbook
General Foods, 1932, 370 pp, hb **$12.00**
General Foods Kitchen Cookbook
1959, 426 pp, hb **$9.00**
George Bernard Shaw Vegetable Cookbook
A. Laden, 1971, 117 pp, hb **$2.00**
German and Viennese Cookbook
Culinary Arts Institute, 1956, 68 pp **$2.00**
German Cooking
R. Howe, 1957, 223 pp **$4.00**
Gifts from our Kitchen
C. Laklan, 1955, 256 pp, hb **$5.00**
Gillette American Cookbook
1889, 521 pp **$10.00**
Girl Scout Cookbook
1971, 160 pp, hb **$3.00**
Give 'em Home Baked Treats . . .
Swans Down, 1945, Kate Smith cover **$5.00**
Given's Modern Encyclopedia of Cooking
1947, 1,724 pp, hb **$15.00**

Giving Delicacy & Flavor to Your Daily Cooking
Rumford, 1932, 32 pp $2.00
Glenna Snow's Cookbook
Snow, 1938, 396 pp, 1st edition $20.00
Glorious Eating for Weight Watchers
Wesson, 1961, 95 pp, pb $4.50
Going Bananas
Feldman, 1978, 112 pp, pb $5.00
Gold Cross Milk
1938 .... $5.00
Gold Medal Flour Cook Book
Washburn Crosby Co., 1917, 74 pp, pb $16.00
Gold Medal Flour Cookbook
1904 .... $18.00
Gold Medal Flour Cookbook
1910 .... $15.00
Gold Medal Flour
Give away, 1917 .... $7.50
Gold Medal Jubilee Recipes
1955, pb $7.50
Gold Medal Sandwich Book
Dedicated to the Earl of Sandwich, 35 pp, lf $2.50
Gold Mine in Your Kitchen
Scott, ca. 1960, 180 pp, hb $4.00
Golden Rule Cookbook
I. Allen, 1916, 128 pp, pb $25.00
Golden Shield Cookbook
Dudley & Co., Fairport, NY, 20 pp $7.00
Golden Treasure of Cooking
Better Homes & Gardens, 1973, 302 pp, hb $6.50
Golfers' Cookbook
Iarrobino, 1968, 91 pp $2.00
Gone with the Wind Famous Southern Recipes Cookbook
Pebeco Toothpaste $35.00
Good Food & How to Cook It
A. Seranne, 1972, 282 pp $10.00
Good Food for Bad Stomachs
Jordan, 1956, 25 pp $5.00
Good Food on a Budget
Better Homes & Gardens, 1971, 96 pp $2.00
Good Housekeeping
1927, red plaid cover $10.00
Good Housekeeping Book of Cookies
Pb $4.00
Good Housekeeping Book of Meals
1927, 256 pp, hb $17.00
Good Housekeeping Book of Menu Recipes
1922, 253 pp, hb $8.50

Gold Medal Flour Cook Book
Published by Washburn Crosby Company
Copyright 1917

Good Housekeeping Cookbook
1944, 981 pp $18.00
Good Housekeeping Cookbook
1963, 803 pp $8.50
Good Housekeeping Cookbook
Marsh, 1935, 254 pp, 4th edition $16.50
Good Housekeeping Cool Drinks
1958, 68 pp $3.00
Good Housekeeping Fish & Shellfish
1958, 67 pp $4.00
Good Housekeeping Party Pie Book
1958, 67 pp $3.50
Good Housekeeping Salads
1958, 68 pp $3.00
Good Housekeeping - Meat Cookbook
1958, 68 pp, pb $2.00
Good Housekeeping - New Ways to Handle Housework
1924 ....$8.50
Good Luck Margarine
1933, 31 pp, sm lf $4.00
Good Luck Recipes
I. Allen, Jelke, 1916, 64 pp, pb $5.00
Good Meals and How to Prepare Them
K. Fisher, 1927, 256 pp, hb $18.00
Good Neighbor Recipes
M. Ericson, 1952, 403 pp $5.00
Good Pies Easy to Make
3rd edition $4.50
Good Pies Easy to Make
Merrell-Soule, ca. 1910, 24 pp, lf $8.00
Good Recipes for Beech-Nut Macaroni
Ca. 1920, lf $2.00
Good Salad Book
M. Barrows, 1952, 189 pp, hb $7.00
Good Things to Cook and How To
Westinghouse, J. Kiene, 142 pp $1.50
Good Things to Eat and How to Prepare
Larkin, 1906, 69 pp, pb $10.50
Good Things To Eat
Arm & Hammer, 1924, 32 pp, lf..$4.00
Good Things To Eat
Cow Baking Soda, 1936, 32 pp..$3.00
Good Things To Eat
Delmonte, 1917, lf..$4.00
Good Things To Eat
M. Anderson, 1937, 15 pp, lf $3.50
Good Things To Eat
M. Anderson, 1940, 15 pp, lf $3.00

Good Meals and How To Prepare Them
A Guide to Meal-Planning, Cooking and Serving
Katharine A. Fisher, Director
Good Housekeeping Institute

Good Things to Eat
Made with
Arm & Hammer Baking Soda
78th Edition

Some Of My Favorite Good Things to Eat
by Martha Lee Anderson

Good Things To Eat
Wesson Oil, 1925, 33 pp, pb $2.50
Good Things To Eat . . . with Bread
Fleischmann, 1916, pb $10.00
Good Things To Eat . . . with Bread
Fleischmann, 1912, 16 pp, pb $5.00
Good Times - Great Recipes
Brockport High School, NY SADD, 64 pp, pb $3.50
Gorton - Codfish Recipes
Gorton Pew, 1906, lf.. $4.00
Gourmet Cooking by the Clock
W. Wayner, 1963, 315 pp, pb $3.00
Gourmet Cooking School Cookbook
D. Lucas, 1964, 336 pp, hb $10.00
Gourmet Food
Culinary Arts, 1955, 68 pp, pb $3.00
Gourmet Magazine
1948 issues .... $6.00 each
Gourmet Magazine
1950's issues... $4.00 each
Gourmet's Almanac
S. MacDougall, 1931, 1st edition $37.50
Gourmet's Basic French Cookbook
L. Diat, 1962, 654 pp $15.00
Gourmet's Guide to New Orleans
N. Scott, 1933, 96 pp, pb.. $9.00
Gourmet's Guide to New Orleans
Scott, 1936, 111 pp, pb $10.00
Grand Isle Cook Book
Ladies Aid, Grand Isle, VT, 1926, 115 pp, pb $7.00
Grand Rapids Cookbook
1916, 260 pp, 2nd edition $12.00
Grand Union Cookbook
M. Compton, 1902, 322 pp $22.50
Grandma's Old Fashioned Molasses
1931, 34 pp, pb $6.00
Granite Ironware Cookbook
1887 .... $90.00
Grannie's Remedies
M. Thomas, 1965, hb.. $4.00
Granulated Gelatine Cookbook
1915, Chalmers $5.00
Gravenhurst Ladies Cookbook
1900, 82 pp $14.00
Graymoor's Treasury of Meatless Recipes
Smaridge, 1965, 72 pp... $3.50
Great American Food Almanac
I. Chalmers, 1986, 230 pp $1.00

AUGUST 1948 • THIRTY-FIVE CENTS

Gourmet
The Magazine of Good Living
August 1948

Gourmet's Guide to New Orleans
By Natalie Scott and Caroline Merrick Jones
Copyright 1933

Great Dishes of The World
R. Carrier, 1964, 280 pp, hb $9.00
Great Ground Beef Recipes
Family Circle, 1966, 168 pp, pb $1.00
Great Northwest Meats
M. Rogers, ca. 1960, 124 pp, pb $4.00
Great Products of Corn
67 pp, lf $2.50
Greater American Cookbook
R. Berolzheimer, 1941 .... $8.00
Green Mountain Cookbook
1941, 90 pp $12.50
Green Thumb Preserving Guide
Anderson, 1976, 244 pp, hb $5.00
Grey Poupon Recipe Book
Ca. 1940, lf $1.00
Grow What You Eat
Planet Jr., 1943, 32 pp $3.00
Guide to Better Foods
Westinghouse, 1930, 40 pp, lf $1.50
Guide to New England Dining
R. Noble, 1957, 63 pp, pb $3.00
Gun Club Cookbook
C. Browne, 1931, 289 pp, hb $10.00

Hamburger & Hot Dogs
Good Housekeeping, 1958, 68 pp, pb **$2.00**
Handbook for Holiday Cuisine
M. Happel, 1970, 397 pp **$3.00**
Handbook for Menu Planning
Gatchell, 1927, 155 pp **$9.50**
Handwritten
Ca. 1900, 30 pp, hb (very poor condition) **$4.00**
Handwritten
Ca. 1900, 30 pp, hb (good condition, leather bound) **$8.00**
Handwritten
Ca. 1930, 30 pp, hb **$3.00**
Hannaford Cook Book
Presbyterian Aid Society, ND, ca. 1900, 58+ pp **$9.00**
Happy Holidays - Goodies for Giving
J. Ashley, lf **$1.00**
Hare Krishna Cookbook
1973, 77 pp, pb **$3.50**
Harper's Universal Recipe Book
1869, 288 pp **$9.00**
Harvard Dames Cookbook
1951, 199 pp, pb **$5.00**
Hawaiian Cuisine
C. Tuttle, 1963, 79 pp, pb **$4.50**
Health Cookbook
P. Bragg, 1937, 205 pp **$10.00**
Health Food Cookbook & Menus
P. Bragg, 1947, 402 pp **$5.00**
Health Giving Dishes
E. Arnold, 1952, 239 pp **$6.00**
Health Giving, Life Saving
"No CB," Tobe, 1973, 816 pp **$22.50**
Heckers Household Hints #2
Pb, red cover **$2.00**

ᘒ

*In 1869, H.J. Heinz's horseradish was in glass jars on
your grocer's shelf.*

ᘒ

Heinz
1939, 210 pp **$10.00**
Heinz
Figural pickle, pb **$5.00**
Heinz Book of Meat Cookery
Heinz, 1930, 54 pp, pb **$5.00**

Heinz Book of Salads
Copyright 1925

Heinz Book of Salads
1925, 95 pp, pb $8.00
Heinz Book of Salads
1934, pb $6.00
Heinz Salad Book
J. Gibson dir., ca. 1933, 99 pp, pb $10.00
Helen Corbitt's Cookbook
1957, 388 pp, hb $6.00
Hellman's
1930 .... $5.00
Heloise's Housekeeping Hints
1965, 166 pp, pb $1.50
Helps for the Hostess
Campbell's Kids wearing top hat, 64 pp $8.00
Herb & Spice Sampler
Davis, 1967 .... $5.00
Herb Cookery
A. Hooker, 1974, 192 pp $5.00
Herbalist Almanac
D. Meyer, 1977, 256 pp, hb $12.00
Here Let Us Feast
M. Fisher, 1946, 491 pp $14.00
Hershey's Favorite Recipe
1970, 32 pp, lf $2.00
Hershey's Recipes
1930 .... $8.00
High Street Cookbook
Hood Sasp, 31 pp, no cover, pb $3.00
Highland Book of Selected Maple Recipes
Carrie Maple Sugar, 1927 .... $4.00
Highlander's Cookbook
Recipes from Scotland, Cameron, 1966, 107 pp $8.00
Hints to Housekeepers
Dr. Miles, lf $3.00
Holiday Book of Food & Drink - Famous Recipes
1952 .... $8.00
Holiday Candy & Cookie Cook Book
J. DeGros, 1954, 14 pp $8.00
Holiday Cookbook
Culinary Arts, 1955, 68 pp, pb $2.00
Holland's Southern Cookbook
1952, 311 pp $6.00
Hollywood Glamour Cookbook
M. Hayes, 1940 .... $3.00
Home Baking Made Easy for Beginners & Experts
Spry, 1953, 25 pp, pb $2.50
Home Book of French Cookery
G. Carter, 1950, 256 pp $7.00

Hershey's 1934 Cookbook
Revised, Copyright 1971

Home Comfort Cookbook
Wrought Iron Range, 1925 .... $20.00
Home Comfort Range Company
1951, lf $5.00
Home Cook Book
E. Ives, 1928, 750 pp, hb $18.00
Home Help
S. Rorer, 1900, 90 pp $5.00
Home Kitchen
A. Barry, 1932, 124 pp, hb $7.00
Home Made Candies and Dainty Dishes
Baker's Chocolate, 1923, lf $4.00
Home Queen Cookbook
1898, 608 pp, hb $25.00
Homemade Breads, Rolls and Kuchens
RG&E NY, 31pp .... $ .50
Homemade Cookies
Farm Journal, 1979, 320 pp $6.00
Homemakers Exchange Recipes
1949, 40 pp, lf $3.00
Homemakers Handbook
D. Myerson, 1939, 576 pp $18.00
Homemakers Prize Recipes
G. Rector, 47 pp $1.00
Hometown Recipes from Worchester NY
Ca. 1978, pb $3.50
Hood's Apothecaries Company Cookbook
1879 .... $15.00
Hood's Book of Homemade Candies
1905, 17 pp, pb $12.00
Hood's Cookbook #1
Hood's Sarsaparilla, 1879, 32 pp, pb $12.00
Hood's Cookbook #2
Hood's Sarsaparilla, 16 pp, pb $5.00
Hood's Cookbook #3
Hood's Sarsaparilla, 31 pp, pb $5.00
Hood's Practical Cookbook
1897, hb $15.00
Horn of Plenty
P. Harvey, 1964, 272 pp $7.00
Hors d'oeuvres
Rochester Science Center NY, 1977, 219 pp, pb $5.00
Hors d'oeuvres and Appetizers
Swartz, 1967, 61 pp, hb $4.00
Hors d'oeuvres & Canapes
J. Beard, 1946, 189 pp, hb $5.00
Horsford Almanac & Cookbook
1886, 36 pp $3.00

Hostess Cookbook
Betty Crocker, 1965, 168 pp.. $8.00
Hotel St. Francis Cookbook
G. Hirdzler, 1919... $20.00
House & Gardens New Cookbook
1967, 390 pp $12.00
Household Cookbook
E. Lord, 1936, 1st edition $12.00
Household Discoveries
S. Morse, 1917, 842 pp, hb $15.00
Household Discoveries & Mrs. Curtis Cookbook
1908, 1,205 pp $22.00
Household Discoveries & Mrs. Curtis Cookbook
1914, 1,205 pp, hb $12.00
Household Recipes
First Presbyterian Church, Mass., ca. 1920, 162 pp+ $7.00
Household Receipts
J. Burnett, 10th edition, pb... $7.50
Household Science and Arts
J. Morris, 1913, 255 pp, hb.. $10.00
Household Searchlight Recipe Book
1935 .... $12.00
Housekeeping in Old Virginia
J. Morton, 1879 .... $98.00
Housekeeping
Robinson, 1980, 1st edition.. $20.00
Housewife Year Book
Kellog, 1937, 36 pp, lf... $5.00
How America Eats
C. Paddleford, 1960.. $27.50
How and Why of Canning
C. Weyant, 54 pp $3.00
How Famous Chef's Use Marshmallow
Angelus Campfire, 1930, pb $9.00
How I Cooked It
B. McDonald, 1949, 256 pp $6.50
How MaMa Could Cook
Wyn, 1946, 178 pp $8.00
How Phyllis Grew Thin
L. Pinkham, 32 pp, lf... $3.50
How to Bake Ration Book
Swans Down, 1923, 23 pp, pb $2.00
How to Barbecue
Test Institute, NY, 15 pp, lf $1.00
How to Beat Those Cordon Bleu's
R. Leinwand, 1974, 288 pp, hb... $6.50
How to Become a Successful Hostess
C. Clark, 1930 .... $8.50

How to Cook a Wolf
Fisher, 1943 ....$12.00
How to Cook Fish
1936, pb $22.00
How to Cook Meat
RG&E NY, 30 pp $1.00
How to Cook With Budweiser
Anheuser Busch, 1952, 34 pp $28.00
How to Eat Better for Less Money
J. Beard, 1954, 316 pp...$8.00
How to Get Children to Eat
G. Langdon, 1938 ....$3.00
How to Have the Most Fun With Cake Mixes
Betty Crocker, 33 pp, pb $5.00
How to Make Candies
Culinary Arts, 1983, 78 pp, hb...$3.00
How to Make Jams, Jellies & Marmalade
Certo, 1927, pb $5.00
How to Make Perfect Cakes
T. Faulds $5.00
How to Take a Trick a Day
Bisquick, 1935, 38 pp $7.50
How's & Why's of Cooking
1936, 252 pp $6.00
Hummingbirds and Radishes
F. Hoffman, 1953, 214 pp $5.00
Hung, Strung & Potted
S. Booth, 1971, 238 pp..$10.00
Hungarian Cookbook
Culinary Arts, 1956, 68 pp, pb $3.00
Hungarian Cookery Book
K. Gundel, 1958, 114 pp..$47.50
Hunter's Stew & Hangtown Fry
L. Perl, 1977, 156 pp $5.00

I Hate to Cook Book, Appendix
P. Bracken, 1966, 1st edition **$10.00**
I Hate to Cook Book
P. Bracken, 1960 .... **$5.00**
I'll Take The Krums
Bond Bread, 1935, pb **$5.00**
Ice Cream
H. Walden, 1983, 160 pp, hb **$13.00**
Ice Cream & Cook Drinks
Good Housekeeping, 1958, 68 pp, pb **$2.00**
Ida B. Allen's Wines & Spirits Cookbook
1934, 366 pp, hb **$3.50**
Ideal Cookery Book - 1,349 Recipes
1891, 402 pp **$30.00**
Ideas for a Refreshment Room
Hotel Press, 1923, 376 pp, hb.. **$15.00**
Illustrated Library of Cooking - Volume I
Family Circle, 1972, 127 pp, hb **$1.50**
In a Copper Kettle
Armstrong, 1958, 116 pp, signed, hb **$5.00**
Incredible Edibles
Lake Forest Park, Washington, 1979, 124 pp, pb **$4.50**
Indiana Farmers Guide New Cookbook
Huntington, Indiana, pb **$12.50**
Instant Baby Food
L. Macdonald, 1975, 12 pp, pb **$1.50**
Institute Cookbook
H. Cramp, 1913, 507 pp+, hb **$10.00**
International Cookbook
Hardin, 1920 .... **$20.00**
International Cookbook
Heywood, 1929, 304 pp **$12.00**
Introduction to Cooking with Amana Radar Range
1980, 303 pp **$5.00**
Irish Country House Cooking
R. Tinne, 1976, 222 pp, hb **$4.00**
Irvin Cobb's Own Recipe Book
1936, 51 pp, lf **$3.00**
It's a Picnic!
N. McIntyre, 1969 .... **$5.00**
It's All in Knowing How
Arm & Hammer, 1935, 37 pp, lf... **$2.00**
Italian Cookbook
M. Taglienti, 1955, 309 pp **$7.00**
Italian Cooking Made Easy
T. Kaufman, 1964, 220 pp, pb **$3.00**

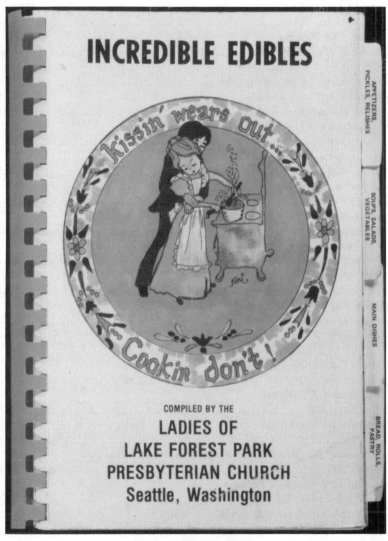

Incredible Edibles
Compiled by the
Ladies of Lake Forest Park Presbyterian Church
Seattle, Washington

Jack Sprat Cookbook
P. Zane, 496 pp, 1973, hb $10.00
Jack's Manual Drink Recipes
1908, 85 pp $12.00
James Beard's Menu for Entertaining
1965, 365 pp, hb $8.50
Jeane Dixon's Astrological Cookbook
1976 .... $4.50

∽

In 1845, Peter Cooper invented a gelatin dessert, but failed to find a market for it until a cough syrup manufacturer advertised it, calling it Jell-o. Elizabeth King was the original Jell-o girl.

∽

Jell-o
George Washington on cover $12.50
Jell-o
Kewpie cover $30.00
Jell-o
M. Parrish illustrated, King & Queen might eat, 1921 .... $45.00
Jell-o
Norman Rockwell illustrated $20.00
Jell-o 1917
20 pp, lf $7.00
Jell-o 1925
Railroad, Leroy, NY, 18 pp, lf $7.00
Jell-o 1932
Lf $5.00
Jell-o 48 Recipes - Want Something Different
23 pp $3.00
Jell-o - America's Most Famous Dessert
Bride on cover, 1916, lf $40.00
Jell-o - America's Most Famous Dessert
Leroy, NY $12.50
Jell-o Dainty Desserts
Janes, pb $12.50
Jell-o Delicious & Beautiful Desserts
Ca. 1909, library slip $3.00
Jell-o Girl Entertains
Rose O'Neil illustrated $30.00
Jell-o Girl Gives a Party
Rose O'Neil illustrated, lf $25.00
Jell-o - Greater Jell-o Recipe Book
1931, 47 pp $7.00

Delicious and Beautiful Jell-o Desserts

Jell-o Ice Cream Powder

The Jell-o Girl Entertains

Jack & Mary's Jell-o Recipe Book

Jell-o Ice Cream Powder
Ca. 1905, lf $10.00
Jell-o Ice Cream Powder
Ca. 1910, library slip.. $3.00
Jell-o - Jack Benny & Mary's
1937, pb $15.00
Jell-o - Joys of Jell-o
1963, 95 pp, lf $1.00
Jell-o - New Jell-o Book of Surprises
1930, 23 pp, lf $6.00
Jell-o - New Jell-o Recipes
1926, 18 pp, lf $7.00
Jell-o - Now Jell-o Tastes Twice as Good
1934, 23 pp $7.00
Jell-o - Polly put the Kettle On
1923, M. Parrish illustrated $65.00
Jell-o Secrets for Automatic Refrigerators
1929, lf... $6.00
Jell-o - Thrifty Jell-o Recipes
1931, 23 pp, lf $5.50
Jell-o - Thru the menu with Jell-o
1927 .... $4.00
Jell-o Today - What Salad, What Dessert, etc.
1926, 32 pp $12.50
Jell-o - What Mrs. Dewey did with the New Jell-o
1933, 23 pp, lf $10.00
Jennie Junes American Cookery Book
J. Croly, 1868 .... $50.00
Jenny Wren Self Rising Flour
Lf $3.00
Jericho Fellowship Church Cookbook
NY, 1982, 72 pp $3.00
Jersey Lily Flour Cookbook
1911 .... $7.00
Jessie Deboth Cookbook
1940, 192 pp, hb $4.50
Jewel Tea Cookbook
Ca. 1940.. $10.00
Jewel Tea
M. Dunbar, 1933 .... $18.00
Jewish Cookbook
Bellin, 1948, 455 pp.. $10.00
Jim Beard's Complete Cookbook for Entertaining
1954 .... $3.50
Jolly Times Junior Recipes
Pb... $10.00
Joy of Cooking
Rombauer & Becker, 1953, 1,013 pp $18.00

Joy of Cooking was first published in 1931.

Joy of Cooking
Rombauer, 1963, 1,013 pp, hb $15.00
Joyce Chen Cookbook
P. White, 1962, 221 pp $5.00
Joys of Cooking
Rombauer, 1946 ....$20.00
Joys of Jell-o
Ca. 1970, 95 pp $2.00
Joys of Jewish Cooking
S. Longstreet, 1978, 1st edition $7.50
J.R. Watkins Co.
1936, hb $5.00
June Platt's Plain & Fancy Cookbook
1941, 356 pp $6.00
Junket Book - Cool Creamy Desserts
1932, 23 pp, pb $4.00
Junket Cooking New York World's Fair
1939, pb $3.00
Just A Few Armour Star Recipes
1930, lf..$3.00
Just A Few Armour Star Bacon Recipes
1920, lf..$2.00
Just A Minute
A. Richardson, 1947, 152 pp $4.00
Just For Two
A. Langdon, 1909, 233 pp $12.00

K-C Baking Powder
   1931 .... **$5.00**
Karo Cook Book
   Hewitt, 1909, 47 pp **$8.50**
Karo Holiday Suggestions
   1980, lf.. **$1.00**
Kate Smith 55 Cake Recipes
   1952, 64 pp, lf **$4.00**
Kate Smith Cookbook
   1940, pb **$25.00**
Kate Smith Favorite Recipes
   Calumet, 1939, 47 pp **$27.00**
Katish, Our Russian Cook
   W. Frolov, 1947, 58 pp **$6.00**
Keep on the Sunny Side of Life
   Kellogg, 1933, 32 pp, lf... **$5.00**
Keep Slim & Trim
   Domino Sugar, 1954, 24 pp, lf.. **$1.00**

W.K. Kellogg's first national advertising campaign for cereal was in 1906.

Kellogg Recipe File Cards
   Blue envelope **$5.00**
Kellogg's Cookbook
   1978 .... **$5.00**
Kelvinator Book of Delicacies
   1926, 23 pp, pb **$2.00**
Kentucky Fare
   M. Bridwell, 1953, 28 pp, pb **$2.00**
Kerr Home Canning Guide
   1945, 14 pp, lf... **$2.00**
Kerr Home Canning
   Chicago World's Fair, 1933, pb **$20.00**
Kerr Home Canning
   Kerr, 1943, 56 pp.. **$15.00**
Kerr Home Canning
   Kerr, 1972, lf **$1.00**
Keynote of Successful Dishes
   Maggi Seasons, 16 pp, lf.. **$2.00**
Kickapoo Indian Medicine Co. Cookbook
   1891 .... **$9.00**

**Keep Slim and Trim With Domino Sugar Menus
Copyright 1954**

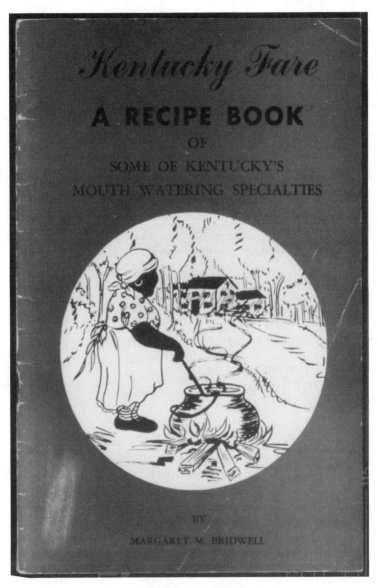

Kentucky Fare
A Recipe Book of
Some of Kentucky's Mouth Watering Specialities
By Margaret M. Bridwell

Kings Bread
18th Century Cooking at Niagara, M. Hallatt, 1986, 56 pp.........**$1.00**
Kingsford Corn Starch Recipe Book
1907 ....**$3.00**
Kitchen Adventures
Eastern Star, D. Clark, signed **$5.00**
Kitchen Sampler
Lakeview Community Church, NY, 1978, pb **$3.50**
Kitchen Tested Recipes
Sunbeam, 1933, 40 pp..**$3.50**
Kitchen Treasures
Milwaukee Journal, 1930, 153 pp **$15.00**
Kitchen Wisdom
F. Arkin, 1977, 260 pp, pb **$2.50**
Kitchenette Cookery
New York Edison Co., 1922, 31 pp, pb **$4.50**
Knights of the Dinner Table
LFP High School, Washington, 75 pp, pb **$3.00**
Knox Dainty Desserts for Dainty People
1915, 41 pp, lf **$6.00**
Knox Dainty Desserts, Candies & Salads
1931 ....**$5.00**
Knox Gelatin Recipes
1896, Black person on cover **$25.00**
Knox Gelatin Recipes
1914 ....**$10.00**
Knox Gelatin Recipes
1936, 55 pp, lf..**$8.00**
Knox Gelatin Recipes
1952, 38 pp **$1.00**
Knox Gelatin Salads, Desserts
1925, 27 pp, pb **$3.00**
Knox Gelatin Desserts, Salads, Candies & Frozen Dishes
1933, 75 pp, lf **$7.50**

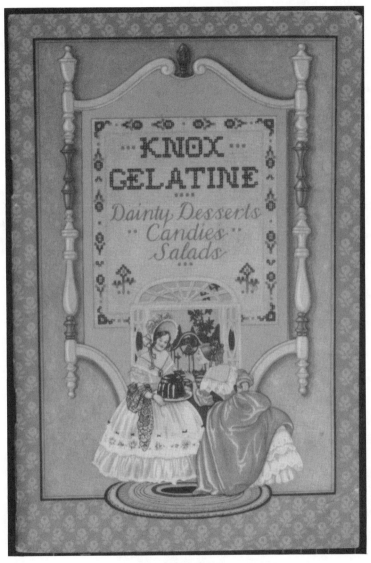

Knox Gelatine
Dainty Desserts, Candies, Salads
Copyright 1931

La Bonne Cuisine Chez Sol
Paris, 1950, 319 pp $7.00

La Bonne Cuisine, de Madame St. Ange
1938, Paris, 445 pp $6.00

La Cuisine Creole
L. Hearn, 1885, 1st edition $600.00

La Cuisine de France
C. Turgeon, 1944, 709 pp $13.00

La Cuisine; Sec. of Modern French Cooking
R. Oliver, 1974, 893 pp, hb $19.00

Ladies' Aid Cookbook
Vaughan, 1971, 186 pp $6.50

Ladies' Aid Society
Lancaster, NY, 1932-1935, lf ....$3.00 each

Ladies' Delight Cookbook, #1
Sulpher Bitters, 1886, 31 pp $10.00

Ladies' New Book of Cookery
S. Hale, 1852, 404 pp, 5th edition $40.00

Ladies Who Lunch - Easy Elegant Recipes
A. Reed, 1972, 174 pp, hb $5.00

Larkin Company Cookbook
1908 ....$12.00

Latest Cake Secrets
Swans Down, ca. 1930, 64 pp $5.50

Laura Secord Canadian Cookbook
1966, 192 pp $13.00

Le Patissier Royal Parisian
Careme, 1815, signed, sold at auction $3,575.00

Leftovers - 500 Delicious Dishes
Culinary Arts, 1954, pb $4.50

Leone's Italian Cookbook
Leone, 1967, 244 pp $5.00

Lessons in Cookery - Book 2
Stewart, 1919, 257 pp $8.00

Let's Cook It Right
A. Davis, 1947, 626 pp, hb $8.50

Let's Cook Outdoors
1959, 63 pp $2.50

Let's Eat Out
Betty Crocker, 27 pp, lf $1.00

Let's Eat
1931 ....$8.25

Let's Enjoy Eating
Wesson Oil, 1932, 48 pp $10.00

Libby's Evaporated Milk Recipes
Can shaped, lf $5.00

Lippincott's Housewifery
L. Balderston, 1919...$35.00
Little Book of Excellent Recipes
Davis Mystery Chef, 1932, 90 pp, pb $5.00
Little Book of French Cooking
Bouquet Garni, 1945, 96 pp...$8.00
Little Cook Book for a Little Girl
1905, 179 pp $10.00
Little Cookbook for a Little Girl
Benton, 1921, 179 pp $9.50
Little Daisy Salad Book
M. Weber, 1923, 24 pp, lf $2.00
Little House Cookbook
B. Walker, 1979, 240 pp, hb $7.00
Little Red Devil Recipes
Underwood, ca. 1920..$4.50
Live Longer Now Cookbook for Joy, Health & Life
J. Leonard, 1977, 368 pp $7.50
Live the Easy Way
WHLD Nia. Hudson, 1947, 24 pp, pb $3.00
L.L. Bean Game & Fish Cookbook
A. Cameron, 1983, 475 pp, hb...$12.00
Loaves and Fishes
M. Kinard, 1978, 219 pp $2.00
Log Cabin - 24 Ways to Use
Recipe cards $20.00
Log Cabin Syrup
1929...$5.00
Log Cabin Syrup
Towle's, set of 24 recipe cards $35.00
Lorain Cooking
Stove co., 1927, 165 pp $8.00
Los Angeles Cookery
Ladies Aid Society, 1881, sold at auction $6,050.00
Love & Dishes
Quattrociocchi, 1950, 416 pp $8.00
Love in the Afternoon Cookbook
ABC TV, 160 pp...$4.00
Low Calorie Cookbook
1951, 253 pp, hb $3.00
Low Calorie Cookbook
Betty Crocker, 1978, 72 pp, pb...$1.00
Low Calorie Desserts
Better Homes & Gardens, 1972, 96 pp $2.50
Low Calorie Menus for Entertaining
B. Ross, 1970, 220 pp $3.00
Low Calorie Recipes
Culinary Arts, 1955, 68 pp, pb...$3.00

Low Fat Cookery
Stead, 1959 .... $6.00
Low Sodium Cook Book
Payne, 1953 .... $12.00
Low Sodium, Fat-controlled Cookbook
Payne, 1960 .... $3.00
Lowney's Cook Book
Lowney's Chocolate, 1912, 421 pp, hb $24.00
Luchow's German Cookbook
J. Mitchell, 1952, 224 pp, hb $15.00
Lum & Abner's 1937 Family Almanac
Horlick's Malted Milk, 1936, 32 pp $5.00
Lutes - Book of Recipes
1936, 213 pp, hb $5.50

ᘒ **M** ᘒ

Ma's Cookin' Mountain Recipes
Sis & Jake, 1966, 55 pp, pb $2.00
Made over Dishes
Mrs. Roher, 1912, 110 pp, hb $2.00
Magic Chef Cooking
America Stove, 1937, 200 pp, hb $10.00
Magic Entrees to Make with Canned Salmon
C. Evans, 1937, 32 pp, lf $3.00
Magical Desserts with Whip n' Chill
1965, 44 pp, pb $6.00
Majestic Cookstove
1900 .... $12.00
Make It Now - Bake It Later
B. Goodfellow, 1961, 35 pp, pb $1.00
Making Biscuits
Royal Baking Powder, 1924 and 1927, 14 pp, pb $3.00
Making Money in Your Kitchen
Hovey, 1953 .... $4.50
Making Pickles and Relishes at Home
1978, 32 pp, lf $1.00
Malleable Iron Range
Monarch, 1906 .... $25.00
Manischewitz Passover Cookbook
D. Ross, 1969, 186 pp, hb $5.00
Manual of Household & Toliet . . .
J. Beeg, 1889, 251 pp $4.00
Manual of Miracle Cookery
Edison Electric, 1935, 64 pp, pb $3.50
Manual of Canning, Pickling, Preserving
C. Campbell, 1950 .... $5.00
Many Ways for Cooking Eggs
Rorer, 1907 .... $4.00
Mapleine Cookery
Cresent Manf., 56 pp, orange plaid cover, pb $4.00
Margaret Rudkin Pepperidge Farm Cookbook
1963, 450 pp $20.00
Marijuana Food: Marijuana Extract Cooking
W. Drake, 1987, 160 pp, pb $4.00
Marquis de Villemer
Paris 1898, 380 pp $5.00
Marshall Classic Cooking
1959 .... $5.00
Martha Washington Cookbook
M. Kimball, 1940 .... $8.00
Mary Arnold's Century Cookbook
1895 .... $20.00

Ma's Cookin' Mountain Recipes
Spiced with mountain customs, sayings, and superstitions.
Copyright 1966

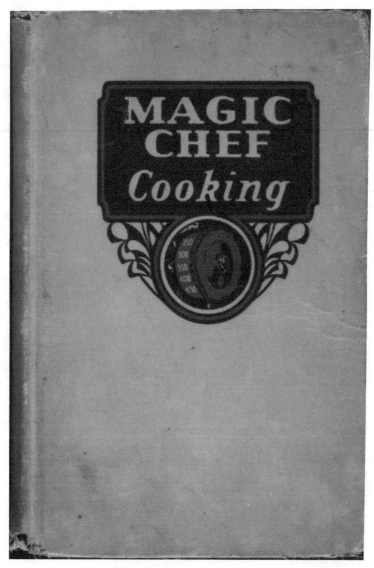

Magic Chef Cooking
Copyright by American Stove Company in 1936

Mary Dunbar's Favorite Recipes
Jewel Tea, 1936, 78 pp **$8.00**
Mary Dunbar's New Cookbook
1933 .... **$15.00**
Mary Ellen's Best of Household Hints
M. Pinkham, 31 pp **$7.00**
Mary Frances' First Cookbook
M. Hays, 1912, 175 pp, hb **$25.00**
Mary Hunt's Pastry & Sweets Diary
1939, 253 pp **$6.50**
Mary Jane's Cookbook
1916, 307 pp, hb **$10.00**
Mary Lee Taylor
Pet Milk, 1949 .... **$4.00**
Mary Meades Country Cookbook
R. Church, 1964, 376 pp **$10.00**
Master Cake Baker
Calumet, 1927 .... **$8.00**
Mastering the Art of French Cooking
J. Childs, 1970, 556 pp+, hb **$15.00**
Maxwell House Coffee Cookbook
1965 .... **$6.00**
Maytag Cookbook
1949, pilgrims on cover, 120 pp, pb **$5.00**
Maytag Dutch Oven Cookbook
49 pp, lf **$8.00**
Mazola Recipes - Corn Products
24 pp, introduction to pure oil from corn, pb **$4.00**
Mazola Salad Bowl
Lf **$3.00**
McCall's Cooking Primer
1953, 48 pp, pb **$2.50**
McMonagle & Rogers Cooking Recipes
1887, Middletown, NY, 44 pp, pb **$7.50**
McNess Almanac
1933, 63 pp **$5.50**
McNess Cookbook
Ca. 1910, 63 pp, pb **$5.00**
McNess Cookbook
Ca. 1935, 79 pp, lady in green **$6.00**
McNess Cookbook
Woman serving man, pb **$10.00**
McNess Recipes Round the World
1908, 63 pp, lf **$8.00**
Meal Time Magic
M. Mitchell, 1951, 120 pp, hb **$2.50**
Meal Time Magic
Taylor, 20 pp, C. Colbert on back **$5.00**

H.W. McNess Cook Book

Meals at Their Best
M. Taylor, 1939 .... **$2.50**
Meals for Small Families
J. Mowat, 1929, 188 pp, hb **$9.00**
Meals For Three
T. Knox, 1932, 32 pp, pb.. **$3.00**
Meals for Two Cookbook
1954 .... **$4.50**
Meals Men Like
M. Taylor, Pet Milk, 15 pp **$3.00**
Meals Planning Guide
1943, 67 pp, Santa on cover, lf **$2.00**
Meals Tested, Tasted and Approved
Good Housekeeping, 1930, 256 pp, hb **$5.00**
Meat 250 Ways
Culinary Arts, 1954, 48 pp... **$4.50**
Meat for Every Occasion
Buff Currier, NY, 1933, 32 pp **$2.00**
Meat Recipes 'Round the World
National Livestock, 1956, 40 pp, pb **$1.50**
Meatless Cooking - Pegeens Vegetarian Recipes
P. Fitzgerald, 207 pp **$5.00**
Mellin's Food Babies
Newton Selover on inside cover **$3.50**
Melrose Honey of Roses
S. Graham, 1942, 95 pp **$15.00**
Men in Aprons
Keating, 1944, 186 pp **$5.00**
Mendelsohn Club Cookbook
1909, 339 pp **$20.00**
Mentha-col Cookbook
Mammy on cover, 1881, 21 pp... **$40.00**
Mentha-col For Southern Housewives
1921, 21 pp **$38.00**
Mentha-col Successful Cooking Recipes
1921 .... **$38.00**
Menu and Recipes for Royal Quick Setting Gelatin
1930, pb **$5.00**
Menus for Everyday of the Year
1954, pb **$4.50**
Meta Given's Modern Encyclopedia of Cooking
J. Ferguson, 1959, 735 pp **$10.00**
Metropolitan Cookbook
1918, 62 pp **$6.00**
Metropolitan Cookbook
1922, lf.. **$5.00**
Metropolitan Cookbook
1953, 56 pp **$2.50**

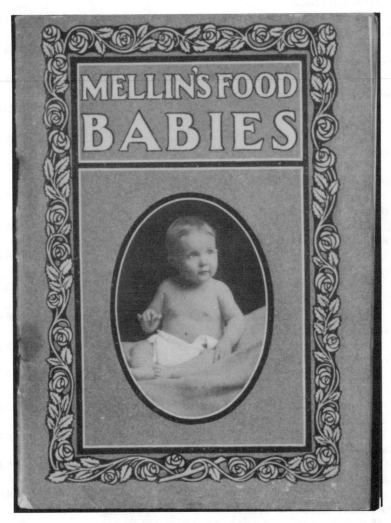

Mellin's Food Babies

Metropolitan Cookbook
1964, 64 pp **$1.00**
Metropolitan Cookbook
Metropolitan Life, 1914, 64 pp, pb **$5.50**
Metropolitan Life
1904 .... **$7.50**
Mexican Cookbook
Sunset, 1971, 96 pp, lf **$4.00**
Mexican Cookery for American Home
Gebhardt, 1923 .... **$8.00**
Mexican Cooking
Culinary Arts, 1976, 96 pp, pb **$1.50**
Mickey Mouse Recipe Card
Ca. 1930 .... **$12.00**
Microwave Cookbook
Betty Crocker, 1981, 288 pp, hb **$8.00**
Microwave Guide & Cookbook
P. Matthews, ca. 1980, 222 pp, hb **$5.00**
Milk and Its Place in Good Cookery
Borden, 1926, 92 pp, hb **$5.50**
Milk, the Way to Health and Beauty
Milk Association, NY, 1939, 55 pp **$3.50**
Minute Tapioca Cookbook
1923, 16 pp, lf **$5.00**
Miracle Meat
M. Taylor, Pet Milk, 1939, 32 pp **$3.50**
Mirro Cook Book
1954 .... **$6.00**
Miss Minerva's Cookbook
Sampson, 1931 .... **$15.00**
Miss Parloa's Cookbook
1881 .... **$30.00**
Mister Peanut's Guide to Nutrition
1970, 32 pp **$4.00**
Modern Approach to Everyday Cooking
1966, 220 pp, hb **$2.00**
Modern Book of Home Canning
C. Schulz, 1978, 191 pp **$5.00**
Modern Cooking
M. Wilson, 1920, 409 pp **$15.00**
Modern Encyclopedia of Cooking
M. Givens, 1955, 733 pp, hb, 2 volume set **$18.00**
Modern Family Cookbook
1942, 938 pp **$12.00**
Modern Family Cookbook
M. Given, 1953, 606 pp **$6.00**
Modern French Culinary Art
Pelaprat, 1966, 1st edition **$25.00**

Metropolitan Cook Book
Metropolitan Life Insurance Company

Modern Guide to Home Canning
Natl pres. cook., ca. 1940, 88 pp, pb $3.00
Modern Homemaker Cookbook
McLean, 1950, 311 pp $6.50
Modern Meat Cookbook
J. Frank, 1958, 350 pp, pb $2.50
Modern Menu Magic - Coldspot Recipes
Sears, 31 pp, pb $1.00
Modern Method of Preparing Food
I. Allen, 197 pp, pb $12.00
Modern Priscilla Cookbook
1924 .... $13.50
Modern Swedish Cookbook
Coombs, 1947, 196 pp $9.00
Modern Ways with Ancient Food
Hecker's Farina, 1934, 16 pp, lf $1.50
Monarch Cookbook
1905, hb $12.00
Monarch Electric Cook Book
1928, 28 pp, pb $1.50
Mondale Family Cookbook
Presidential Comm., 1984, 139 pp $6.00
Montclair Gelatin
Sears & Roebuck, tiny recipe, lf $5.00
Moody's Household Advisor & Cookbook
M. Moody, 1884, 1st edition $36.00
Moosewood Cookbook
M. Katzen, 1977, 221 pp, hb $10.00
More Power To You and Victory in '43
Jan. 1943, lf $1.50
Morristown Cookbook
1948, 428 pp, pb $5.00
Most for Your Money Cookbook
B. Brown, 1938, 228 pp, 1st edition $28.00
Mother Barbour's Favorite Recipes
Miles Laboratory $9.00
Mountain Dessert Book
D. Fisher, 1983, 110 pp, hb $7.95
Mr. Ham Goes To Town
Morrell, 1939, 14 pp, lf $1.50
Mrs. Peterson's Simplified Cooking
People's Light and Gas, 1925 .... $11.00
Mrs. Allen on Cooking Menu Service
1924, 929 pp $15.00
Mrs. Allen's Cookbook
Allen, 1922, 724 pp $16.00
Mrs. Beeton's Cookery & Household Management
I. Beeton, 1967, 1,344 pp $15.00

Mr. Ham Goes To Town
John Morrell & Company

Mrs. Beeton's Favorite Recipes
M. Black, 1977, 22 pp, pb $2.00
Mrs. Beeton's Household Management
I. Beeton, 1926 .... $27.50
Mrs. Curtis's Cookbook
1913, 1,173 pp, hb $25.00
Mrs. Hill's Cookbook
1881 .... $75.00
Mrs. Lincoln's Boston Cookbook - What to do and not to do
1886 .... $75.00
Mrs. Ma's Cookbook
N. Ma, 1966, 178 pp, hb $15.00
Mrs. Roger's Cakes & Fillings
Roher, 1905 .... $20.00
Mrs. Roher's New Cookbook
1902, 731 pp $10.00
Mrs. Scott's North American Seasonal Cookbook
A. Scott, 1921 .... $25.00
Mrs. W.H. Wilson New Cookbook
1914 .... $25.00
Mrs. Washington's Sewanee Cookbook
1926, 207 pp $25.00
Mrs. Wilson's Cookbook
M. Wilson, 1920, 487 pp $12.00
Mrs. Winslow's Domestic Receipts for 1867
Lf $8.00
Mrs. Winslow's Domestic Receipts for 1875
32 pp, pb $6.00
Mueller's Macaroni Cookbook
1933 .... $4.00
Mushroom Cookry
R. Reitz, 206 pp, pb $7.50
My Better Homes & Gardens Cookbook
1940, hb $15.00
My Better Homes & Gardens Cookbook
1925, hb $23.00
My Grandmother's Cookery Book
S. Wolley, 1976, 112 pp, pb $5.00
My Own Cookbook - From Stillmeadow & Cape Cod
G. Taber, 1972, 312 pp $15.00
My Own Cookery Book
1923 .... $20.00
Mystery Chef's Own Cookbook
L. Green, 1943, 365 pp $14.00

N.K. Fairbank & Co. Cottolene Shortening
1882 .... **$7.50**

Nancy Drew Cookbook
C. Keene, 1973, 159 pp **$4.50**

National Bisquit Cookbook
1921 .... **$10.00**

National Cookbook
S. Hibben, 1932, 425 pp **$12.00**

National Dessert
Riches Tryphosa, Statue of Liberty cover, lf **$5.00**

National Drink
Welch's, Gibson Girl cover **$5.00**

National Wildlife Cookbook
National Wildlife Federation, 1984, 175 pp, pb **$6.00**

National Yeast Company Cookbook
1886, 47 pp, pb **$4.00**

Naturopathic - Vegetarian Cookbook
1907, 72 pp **$24.00**

Nestle Cookbook
Nestle Co., 184 pp **$3.50**

New American Cookbook
Wallace, 1943, 931 pp **$14.00**

New American Cookbook
Wallace, 1946 .... **$10.00**

New Art of Modern Cooking
General Electric, 1937, 112 pp **$10.00**

New Art of Simplified Cooking
General Electric, 1940, 84 pp, pb **$9.00**

New Banana
United Fruit **$1.50**

New Book of Cake Designs for Bakers
H. Heug, 1893 .... **$35.00**

New Book of Cookery
Fannie Farmer, 1912, 419 pp **$20.00**

New Book of Cookery
Fannie Farmer, 1915 .... **$12.00**

New Butterick Cookbook
1924 .... **$16.00**

New Calumet Baking Book
Parker, 1931, 31 pp, lf **$3.00**

New Can Opener Cookbook
Cannon, 1968, 318 pp, hb **$2.00**

New Century Cookbook
Young ladies working, Pennsylvania, 1901, 160 pp, pb **$12.00**

New Columbian White House Cookery Book
1893 .... **$17.00**

New Cooking Suggestions
Proctor & Gamble, 1928, 19 pp **$3.00**
New Delights from the Kitchen
Kelvinator, 1930, 64 pp **$10.00**
New Delineator Recipes
Ca. 1930, 222 pp **$16.00**
New England Butt'ry Shelf Cookbook
M. Campbell, 1969, 192 pp **$13.00**
New England Cookbook
1906 .... **$20.00**
New England Cookbook
E. Early, 1954, 236 pp **$10.00**
New England Cooking
Culinary Arts, 1953 .... **$3.00**
New England Yankee Cookbook
I. Wolcott, 1939, 398 pp, hb **$8.00**
New Food Book
M. Berger, 1978, 350 pp **$3.00**
New Good and Easy
Betty Crocker, 1962, 192 pp **$8.00**
New Home Cookbook
Illinois State Register, 1925, 128 pp **$8.00**
New Hostess Today
L. Larned, 1917 .... **$20.00**
New Household Discoveries
S. Morse, 1917, 805 pp **$22.00**
New James Beard
J. Beard, 1981, 625 pp, hb **$5.00**
New Jell-O Recipes
1932, lf **$3.25**
New Magic in the Kitchen
Borden, ca. 1942, 175 dishes, 62 pp, pb **$5.00**
New Metro Cookbook
1973, 60 pp, pb **$2.00**
New Operahouse Cookbook
Ladies Seneca Fall, NY, 1912, 56 pp, pb **$12.00**
New Orleans Creole Recipes
M. Brenner, 1955, 86 pp **$8.00**
New Outdoor Cookbook
Betty Crocker, 1971, 160 pp **$5.00**
New Perfection Oil Cook Stove
1922 .... **$10.00**
New Perfection Oil Stove
1914, 27 pp, pb **$15.00**
New Process Cookbook
Stove Co., ca. 1890, 64 pp, pb **$6.00**
New Recipe Book
Junket, 1938 .... **$2.00**

New Cooking Suggestions
Copyrighted 1928 by Proctor & Gamble Co.

New Recipes for Busy-day Meals
M. Taylor, Pet Milk, 15 pp $3.00
New Recipes for Good Eating
Proctor & Gamble, 1949, 112 pp, pb $7.00
New Recipes of Pillsbury Flour
(Form. 1568), lf...$1.50
New Recipes, Crisco
1930, 19 pp, pb $3.25
New Royal Cook Book
Royal Baking Powder, 1920, 49 pp, pb $5.00
New Swans Down Desserts & Hot Breads
1945, lf...$1.00
New System of Domestic Cookery
London, 1849, 348 pp $175.00
New T-Fal French Cookbook
M. Pendergast, 1977, 85 pp $2.00
New Walnut Cookbook
Diamond Walnut, 28 pp, pb $2.00
New Ways to Make Pies & Candies
Knox, 1934, lf $2.00
New York Times 60-Minute Gourmet
P. Franey, 1979, 339 pp $5.00
New York Times Cookbook
C. Clairborne, 1961, 716 pp, 1st edition $15.00
New York Times Natural Foods Cookbook
J. Hewitt, 1971, 434 pp $6.00
New York World's Fair Cookbook
C. Gaige, 1939, 309 pp, hb $26.00
News Cook Book
N. Dorris, ca. 1930, 159 pp, pb $6.00
No Time For Cooking
Arlene Francis, 103 pp, pb $6.00
Norge Recipe Book
Norge, ca. 1930 ....$2.00
North Brother's Ice Cream Freezers
1895 ....$10.00
Not Just a Load of Old Lentiles
R. Elliot, 1972, Eng., 216 pp, pb...................................$4.00
Now Jello Tastes Twice as Good
1934, 22 pp, pb $3.00
Nunsuch Mincesmeat
Ca. 1915, 28 pp $3.00
Nuvel Cuisine of J. Troisgros
1978, 254 pp, hb $4.00
NY Times Large Type Cookbook
J. Hewitt, 1968, 446 pp $8.50
Nyal Drug Store
1916 ....$3.00

New Royal Cook Book
Royal Baking Powder Co., New York, U.S.A.
Copyright 1920

The New York Times Natural Foods Cookbook
By Jean Hewitt

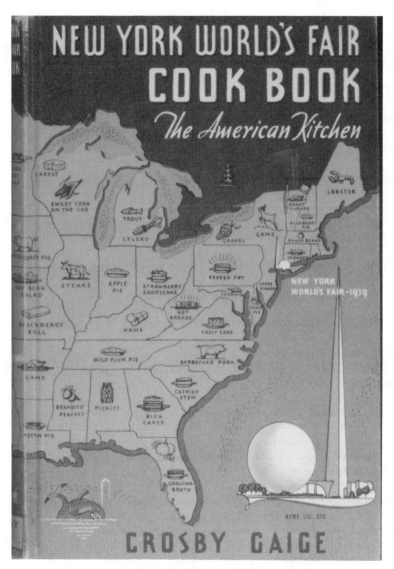

New York World's Fair Cookbook
By Crosby Gaige

O.E.S. Cookbook
Orleans Chapter Eastern Star, NY, 1906, 62 pp, pb **$8.00**
Occident Flour
1936, 24 pp, pb **$5.00**
Of Cabbages & Kings
W. Rhode, 1938 .... **$4.50**
Off My Toes
E. Masterson, 1961 .... **$17.50**
Official 1985 Kentucky State Fair Cookbook
Hamilton, 1986, 440 pp **$8.00**
Old Family Favorites
Eastern Star 1969, 382 pp, pb **$10.00**
Old Fashion Pumpkin Recipes
Bear Wallow, 1979, 31 pp **$3.00**
Old Fashion Molasses Goodies
Brer Rabbit, 1932, 48 pp, pb **$2.50**
Old Mr. Boston
1940, 160 pp, hb **$15.00**
Old Mr. Boston De Luxe Official Bartender's Guide
1956, hb **$5.00**
Old Mr. Boston De Luxe Official Bartender's Guide
1968, 149 pp, hb **$3.00**
Old Shaker Recipes
Bear Wallow, 1982, 30 pp **$3.00**
On the Chafing Dish
1890, H. Bailey, 76 pp, hb, poor condition **$10.00**
On-Camera Recipes
Knox, 1962, 48 pp, pb **$2.00**
Onions Without Tears
J. Bothwell, 1950 .... **$5.00**
Only Love Beats Butter
Land O' Lakes, 33 pp **$1.50**
Oriental Cookbook
Sunset, 1971, 96 pp, lf **$4.00**
Original Boston Cooking School Cookbook
1896, reprint 1980, 1st edition **$9.50**
Oscar of the Waldorf
K. Schriftgiesser, 1943, 248 pp, hb, signed **$8.00**
Our Favorite Recipes
A. Reynolds, NY, ca. 1960, 83 pp, pb **$3.50**
Our Favorite Recipes
LFP Church, Washington, ca. 1950, 65 pp, pb **$5.00**
Out of this World Cookbook
Astronauts Wives, 1978, 171 pp **$6.00**
Out of Vermont Kitchens
Trinity Church, 1949, 400 pp, pb **$7.50**

Outdoor Cooks Bible
  J. Bates, 1963, 212 pp, pb $3.00
Outdoor Picture Cookbook
  B. James, 1954, 126 pp $7.00
OXO Cookbook
  England, 1925, 16 pp, pb $3.00

Pillsbury's Diamond Anniversary Recipes

Pacific Hostess Cookbook
Gary, 1956, 256 pp, hb $7.50

Pack More Manpower Into His Lunchbox
RG&E, Feb. 1943, lf $1.00

Pan American Complete Round The World Cookbook
M. Waldo, 1959, 478 pp $12.00

Pan-Pacific Cookbook
L. McLaren, 1915 .... $35.00

Paper Bag
1910, pb $15.00

Paprikas Weiss Hungarian Cookbook
E. Weiss, 1979, 192 pp, hb $7.00

Paradise Cookbook
C. Tongo, 1957, 96 pp, hb $3.00

Paris Cuisine
J. Beard, 1952, 272 pp, hb $12.00

Party Cheese Recipes
Look Magazine, Jack Benny, lf $1.50

Pasta & Pizza Cookbook
M. Street, 1985, 128 pp, hb $3.00

Pastry and Pies
Home Services, Rochester, NY, 15 pp, pb $1.00

Paul Richards - Pastry Book
1938, 172 pp $14.50

Pearl Baking Powder
Milwaukee, 1890, 192 pp $17.00

Peasant Cookbook
M. Tracy, 1955, 224 pp $6.00

Penguin Cordon Bleu Cookery
R. Hume, 1963, 508 pp, pb $4.00

Pennsylvania Dutch Recipe Book
Pennsylvania Dutch Brand, 1961, 62 pp, pb $2.00

Pennsylvania Dutch Cookbook
C. Davidow, 1972, 62 pp, pb $3.50

Pennsylvania Dutch
Sunbonnet girl cover, 1936, pb $15.00

Pepperidge Farm Cookbook
M. Rudkin, 1963, 440 pp, hb $15.00

Pepsi-Cola Recipe Book
1940, pb $12.00

Personal Recipes of Brer Rabbit
25 pp, New Orleans on cover, pb $3.00

Pet Recipes
Pet Milk, 1930, 80 pp $5.00

Peter Hunt's Cape Cod Cookbook
1954, 174 pp, hb $5.00

Physiology of Taste
Brillat-Savaran, 1926, limited edition, 326 pp, hb **$250.00**
Physical Culture Cookbook
MacFadden, 1924, 1st edition... **$16.00**
Picasso & Pie Buffet Cookbook
Thompson, 1969, 55 pp, hb **$2.00**
Pickle in the Middle
F. Zweifel, 1979, 64 pp, pb **$3.50**
Picture Cook Book
Betty Crocker, 1950, 1st edition **$20.00**
Pies & Pastries - 250 Superb
Culinary Arts, 1954, 48 pp... **$4.50**
Pies a Plenty
Harris, 1940, 206 pp.. **$8.00**
Pies, Waffles, Muffins, Biscuits, Cookies, Swans Down
1929, 16 pp, pb **$2.50**
Pies
Culinary Arts, 1954, 48 pp, pb **$3.00**

*The first Pillsbury Bake-Off was held in 1949. The recipe
book was published in 1950. Mrs. Eleanor Roosevelt and
Duke and Dutchess of Windsor were guest.*

Pillsbury Bake-off
1st, pb **$65.00**
Pillsbury Bake-off
2nd, pb **$15.00**
Pillsbury Bake-off
3rd, 1953, pb... **$15.00**
Pillsbury Bake-off
4th, pb **$11.00**
Pillsbury Bake-off
5th, 1954, 96 pp, pb **$8.00**
Pillsbury Bake-off
6th, 1955, pb... **$10.00**
Pillsbury Bake-off
7th, 98 pp, pb.. **$7.00**
Pillsbury Bake-off
9th, pb **$5.00**
Pillsbury Bake-off
8th, 100 Grand National recipes **$5.00**
Pillsbury Bake-off
13th, pb **$5.00**

FROM PILLSBURY'S

2nd Grand National

$100,000 RECIPE AND BAKING CONTEST

100

Prize-Winning Recipes

25¢

Pillsbury's 2nd Grand National
100-Prize Winning Recipes
Copyright 1951

Pillsbury's Best
10th Grand National Bake-off Cookbook

Pillsbury Bake-off
14th, pb $5.00
Pillsbury Bake-off
18th, 1967, 96 pp, pb $5.00
Pillsbury Bake-off
1968, 145 pp, hb $5.00
Pillsbury Bake-off Cookie Favorites
1969, 64 pp, pb $4.00
Pillsbury Best Cakes
65 pp, ca. 1960, pb $5.00
Pillsbury Butter Cookie
48 pp, pb, ca. 1957 ....$4.00
Pillsbury Cook Book
1911, 125 pp, pb $18.00
Pillsbury Cookbook
1911..$15.00
Pillsbury Cookbook
1914, 122 pp $25.00
Pillsbury Cookbook
1924..$10.00
Pillsbury Cookbook
1941..$6.00
Pillsbury Cookbook
Pillsbury Laboratories, 48 pp, red and cream swirl cover $4.00
Pillsbury Family Cookbook
Ca. 1960, 576 pp $6.00
Pillsbury Recipes - Flour, Oats & Vitos
32 pp $3.00
Pillsbury Silver Anniversary Bake-off
25th, 1974, 92 pp, pb $5.00
Pillsbury Treasury of Bake-off Favorites
....$5.00
Pillsbury's Diamond Anniversary Recipes
1944, pb (see page 137) $8.00
Pinstripe Gourmet
R. Ackart, 1986, 434 pp, pb $8.00
Pita the Great
V. Habeeb, 1986, 176 pp $4.00
Pleasures of Italian Cooking
Salta, 1962, 239 pp...$4.50
Plus Food for Minus Meals
Kellogg, 1940, 16 pp $5.00
Polish Cookery
M. Monatowa, 1958, 314 pp, hb $6.00
Pooh Cookbook
V. Ellison, 1969, 120 pp, hb $4.00
Potato Cook Book - State of Maine
1950, 63 pp, pb $3.00

The Pillsbury Cook Book
Copyright 1911

89¢

Silver *Anniversary*

Bake-Off

Cookbook

Pillsbury

F 06743

100 winning recipes from BAKE-OFF® 25
including the GE Microwave Cooking Award Winner

Silver Anniversary Bake-off Cookbook
Copyright 1974

Potatoe Cookery
A. Glorio, London, 80 pp, hb **$4.00**
Potatoes - 250 Ways of Serving
Culinary Arts, 1954, pb... **$4.50**
Poultry & Game
Good Housekeeping, 1958, 68 pp, pb **$2.00**
Poultry Cooking
USDA, 1941, 33 pp, lf.. **$1.00**
Practical Cookbook Bliss
1887, 1,000 recipes **$25.00**
Practical Cooking & Dinner Giving
M. Henderson, 1881, 376 pp **$25.00**
Practical Cooking & Dinner Giving
M. Henderson, 1888, 376 pp, hb **$6.00**
Practical Cooking and Serving
J. Hill, 1912, 680 pp, hb **$20.00**
Prairie Farmer WLS Cookbook
Centennial edition, Chicago, 1941 .... **$12.50**
Praise the Cook
Pet Milk, 1962, lf.. **$1.00**
Praktische Konditorei-kunst
J. Werber, German, 4th edition, 1921, hb **$300.00**
Preparation of Foods for Your Steinhorst
24 pp, pb **$3.40**
Presenting Knox Cookies
1938, 23 pp, pb **$1.50**
Preserving with Karo
1912, lf.. **$5.00**
President Cookbook
P. Cannon, 1968, 545 pp, hb **$15.50**
Presidential Cookbook
I. McKinley, adapted White House Cookbook, 1900, 440 pp **$25.00**
Presscott Class Recipe Book
Baptish Church, Rochester, NY, 87 pp, pb **$2.00**
Pressure Cookery
L. Carroll, 1947, 171 pp... **$4.00**
Premium Catalogue & Recipe Book
P. Rossi, 1954 .... **$3.00**
Primer for Pickles
R. Guthrie, 1898-1974, pb.. **$4.00**
Prince Golden Macaroni Recipes
1951, 30 pp **$5.00**
Principles & Practice of Butter Making
G. McKay, 1912, 350 pp, hb **$9.50**
Principles of Cookry
A. Barrows, 1910.. **$20.00**
Principles of Domestic Engineering
M. Pattison, 1915 .... **$35.00**

Prize Winning Recipes
Minute Tapicoa, 1927, 32 pp, pb $3.00
Prize Winning Maine Recipes
Boone's Wharf, ca. 1940 .... $3.00
Prize Winning Recipes using Swift Brand Lard
26 pp $1.00
Proven Recipes - Three Great Products from Corn
Indian cover, 66 pp, lf $4.00
Prudence Penny's Cookbook
1939, hb $8.00
Prunes for Epicures
United prunes, 1933, lf $2.00
Pumpkin Cookery
Cobblestone Society, Childs, NY, 1980, 56 pp $3.50
Pure Food Cookbook
M. Maddock, 1914 .... $20.00
Pure Food
1907 .... $8.00
Pyrex Prize Recipes
Corning Glass, 1953, 128 pp $6.00

Proven Recipes
Showing the uses of the Three Great Products from Corn

Q

Quaker Recipes
Woman's Auxiliary, NC, 1954, 198 pp, pb $8.00
Quaker Woman's Cookbook
E. Lea, 1982, 310 pp, hb $8.00
Quality Grocer
March 1931, 24 pp, pb $11.00
Queen is in the Kitchen
McCarthy, 1954, 232 pp, hb $5.00
Querulous Cook
D. Vanetti, 1963, 291 pp, hb $6.00
Quick & Easy Dinners
Sunset, 1970, 96 pp, pb $4.50
Quick & Easy Meals for Two
L. Shouer, 1952, 274 pp, hb $6.00
Quick 'n Easy Riceland Rice
Ca. 1950, lf $1.50
Quick Gourmet Dinners
Rieman, 1972, 141 pp..$6.50
Quick 'n Easy
Good Housekeeping, 1958, 68 pp, pb $2.00

Ralston Mother Goose Recipe Book
  1919, 15 pp, pb $12.00
Ralston Recipes
  1920, 15 pp, woman in shoe, lf..$12.00
Ransom's Family Receipt Book
  1886, 32 pp, pb $8.00
Ransom's Family Receipt Book
  1897, 32 pp, pb $8.00
Ransom's Family Receipt Book
  1904, 32 pp, pb $6.00
Ransom's Family Receipt Book
  1906, 32 pp, pb $4.00
Raw Vegetable Juices
  Walker, 1947, 127 pp $3.00

*Rawleigh's began in 1888 and annually published its
almanac "for gratuitous distribution into rural homes
throughout North America."*

Rawleigh Health Almanac Cookbook
  1927, 32 pp $5.00
Rawleigh's 40th Anniversary
  1929..$4.00
Rawleigh's Almanac Cook Book & Medical Guide
  1916, 99 pp, pb $16.50
Rawleigh's Almanac Cookbook
  1915..$16.00
Recipes & Menus for All Occasions
  Frito Co., 1947, 31 pp, pb $3.00
Recipes - African Cooking
  Time-Life, 1969, pb $6.00
Recipes - America, Eastern Heartland
  Time-Life, 1969, pb $6.00
Recipes - America, Melting Pot
  Time-Life, 1969, pb $6.00
Recipes - America, Northwest
  Time-Life, 1969, pb $6.00
Recipes - America, the Great West
  Time-Life, 1969, pb $6.00
Recipes - American Cooking Southern Style
  Time-Life, 1969, pb $6.00
Recipes - American Cooking, New England
  Time-Life, 1969, pb $6.00

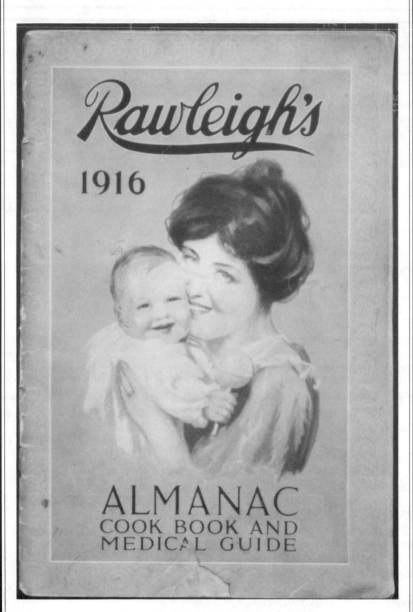

Rawleigh's 1916 Almanac
Cook Book and Medical Guide

*Rawleigh's 1917 Almanac
Cookbook and Medical Guide*

Recipe Book - Beard on Bread
J. Beard, 1974, 230 pp, hb $10.00
Recipe Book for Club Allum
Howlett, 1926, 35 pp, pb $4.00
Recipe Book - Grand Union
1931, 96 pp, pb $4.00
Recipe Cooking in the British Isles
Time-Life, 1969, pb $6.00
Recipe Cooking of Germany
Time-Life, 1969, pb $6.00
Recipe Cooking of Spain & Portugal
Time-Life, 1969, 112 pp, pb $6.00
Recipes - Cream Dove Shortening
14 pp, lf $2.00
Recipes - Creole & Acadian
Time-Life, 1969, pb $6.00
Recipes for Dainty Dishes
Sunkist Lemon, ca. 1900, 40 pp, pb $4.00
Recipes for Del Varitys of Bread
Fleishmann, 1928, 60 pp, pb $3.00
Recipes for Everyday for Oranges & Lemons
64 pp, pb $4.00
Recipes for Fun and Friendship
K. Phillips $1.50
Recipes for Salads
Pompeian Olive Oil, 1913 .... $3.00
Recipes for the Sutterley Chafing Dish
H. Johnson, 1894, 32 pp $15.00
Recipes for Today
General Foods, 1943 .... $2.50
Recipes for Using Canned Food
S. Haskin, 1960, 32 pp, pb $1.00
Recipes for Yeast Raised Breads
Standard Brands, 1940, 10 pp $2.00
Recipes from Historic Long Island
YWCA, 1948, 408 pp $10.00
Recipes - Jelke Good Luck Margarine
1927, 40 pp, pb $3.00
Recipes - Middle East
Time-Life, 1969, pb $6.00
Recipes of Carribean Islands
Time-Life, 1969, pb $6.00
Recipes of Italy
Time-Life, 1969, pb $6.00
Recipes of Latin American
Time-Life, 1969, pb $6.00
Recipes of Quality - A Cook Book Delux
Amer. Brew., 1912, 224 pp, hb $22.00

Recipes of Strong Memorial Hospital
Rochester, NY, 1976, 114 pp, pb $4.00
Recipes Quintet of Cuisine
Time-Life, 1970, 152 pp, pb $6.00
Recipes to Stretch Your Sugar Ration
Arm & Hammer, 1942, lf $5.00
Recipes - Wesson Oil
1913, 48 pp, pb $3.00
Recipes With Good Luck Margarine
Cake cover, lf $1.00
Receipt Book
Carter's Extract, 32 pp, lf $10.00
Record Wartime Cookbook
N. Hitchcock, 1918 .... $12.00
Rector's Naughty '90s Cookbook
A. Kirkland, 1949, 247 pp, hb $17.00
Rector
1928, signed $20.00
Red Flannel Hash & Shoo Fly Pie
L. Perl, 1965, 288 pp, hb $5.00
Refrigerator Desserts - 250 Luscious
Culinary Arts, 1945, pb $4.50
Reliable Recipes - Calumet
Gram at door w/ cal boy, 11th edition, pb $8.50
Reliable Recipes
Reliable Flour, 1904, 32 pp, pb $8.00
Reliable Recipes
Calumet, 1922, 27th edition, 80 pp, lf $9.00
Republican Cookbook
Brownstone Press, 1969, 200 pp $4.50
Rice - 200 Ways to Serve It
Culinary Arts, 1935 .... $4.00
Riceland Cookbook
Lf $2.00
Riches of New Jersey
1952, 32 pp, lf $4.00
Ritzy Rice
M. Street, 1985, 128 pp, hb $4.00
Rival Crock-pot Cooking
M. Neill, 1975, 208 pp $5.00
Rochester Advisory Nutrition Council Menus
Parran, Rochester, NY, 1933, 28 pp $5.00
Rochester Intern Friendship Cookbook
Rochester, NY, 60 pp, pb $3.50
Rockie Mountain Cookery
Norton, 1903 .... $40.00
Rodale Herb Book
W. Hylton, 1974, 633 pp, hb $8.00

Romagnoli's Meatless Cookbook
Romagnoli, 1976, 272 pp, pb **$7.50**
Roman Meal Recipes
Roman Meal, 1932, pb **$3.50**
Romanian Cookbook
A. Stan, 1951, 220 pp, 1st edition **$8.00**
Roughing It Easy
D. Thomas, 1974, 203 pp, pb, signed **$6.00**
Round the World Cookbook
Allen, 1934, hb **$10.00**
Round the World Cookbook
K. Morrow, 64 pp, pb **$5.00**
Round World Cookbook
Waldo, 1954 .... **$5.00**
Royal Baker & Pastry
1911, pb **$20.00**
Royal Baker and Pastry Cookbook
Royal Baking Powder, 1906, lf **$3.00**
Royal Baking Powder
1936, card **$1.50**
Royal Baking Powder
1942, lf **$7.00**
Royal Cookbook
1922, poor condition **$2.00**
Royal Cookbook
1929 .... **$6.50**
Royal Cookbook
1930, 49 pp, pb **$3.00**
Royal Cookbook
1935, 64 pp **$4.50**
Royal Cookbook
1940, red cover, pb **$5.00**
Royal Cream of Tarter
1944, 64 pp, pb **$6.00**
Royal Pudding
Ginger Rogers, 1940 .... **$10.00**
Royal Recipes on Parade
Royal Gelatin, 1942, 48 pp, pb **$6.50**
Royal Success in Baking
Royal Baking Powder, 1942, 22 pp, lf **$3.00**
Rum Connoisseur
Chico, 1944, 44 pp, pb **$1.50**
Rumford Baking Powder Cookbook
1911, 32 pp, girl in green **$17.00**
Rumford Baking Powder
1913, 32 pp, pb **$6.50**
Rumford Cookbook
Fannie Farmer, 1922, plain red and black cover, 46 pp, pb **$8.00**

Royal Cream of Tartar Cookbook
Copyright 1940

Rumford Common Sense Cookbook
1895, 64 pp $8.00
Rumford Complete Cook Book
L. Wallace, 1946, 213 pp, hb $7.00
Rumford Complete Cookbook
L. Wallace, 1918 .... $12.00
Rumford Complete Cookbook
L. Wallace, 1923, 241 pp $12.00
Rumford Complete
L. Wallace, 1928, pb $15.00
Rumford Cook Book
Fannie Farmer, 1906, 47 pp $12.00
Rumford Cookbook
1909, lf, wheat girl $8.00
Rumford Fruit Cookbook
1927, 47 pp, pb $6.00
Rumford Modern Methods of Cooking
Splint, 64 pp, black and red cover $2.50
Rumford Recipes for Biscuits and Rolls
L. Wallace, chart $7.00
Rumford Recipes for Cakes and Cookie Making
1926 .... $12.00
Rumford Receipts
Ca. 1906, pb, poor condition $8.00
Rumford Southern Recipes
M. Wilson, 1894, 65 pp, lf $7.00
Rumford Way of Cooking
J. Hill, 68 pp, (k-71), pb $4.00
Russian Dishes from the Russian Tea Room
Lf $1.00
Russian Jew Cooking in Peru
V. Autumn, 1973, 192 pp, pb, 1st edition $4.00
Russian Tea Room Cookbook
F. Stewart, 1981, 239 pp, hb $3.50
Russian
Printed in USSR, 1953 .... $25.00
Ryzon Baking Book
M. Neil, 1916 .... $10.00

Salad Book
M. Dahnke, 1955, 307 pp, pb $3.00
Salad Leaves
Ivanhoe Mayo, 1939, 36 pp, pb $8.00
Salad Recipes - 500 Delicious
Culinary Arts, 1954, 48 pp, pb $4.50
Salad-ology
Ivanhoe Mayo, 24 pp, lf $2.00
Salads Alluring & New
A. Bradley, 1926, 12 pp, lf $2.00
Salads and Sandwiches
Women's World Magazine, 1924, 48 pp, hb $5.50
Salads, Br. Lunch, Canned Meals
Chicago Press, 1933, 400 pp, hb $16.00
Salads
Home Economics Teachers, 384 pp, pb $6.50
Salads, Sandwiches & Chafing
J. Hill $20.00
Salads, Suppers, Picnics
F. Leggett $2.00
Salads, Tossed and Otherwise
Kraft, lt .... $ .75
Sally Stokely's Prize Recipes
Stokely Foods, 1935 .... $6.00
Sandwich - 500 Tasty
Culinary Arts, 1954, pb $4.50
Santa Christmas Recipes
RG&E, 19 pp $1.00
Sauces, Gravies & Dressings
Culinary Arts, 1954, pb $4.50
Savannah Cookbook
H. Colquitt, introduction Ogden Nash, 1933 .... $10.00
Save Sugar Wheat and Fats
Fleischmann, Nation of Soldiers, pb $3.00
Savory Dishes
Kitchen Bouquet, 1916, lf $2.50
Savory Suppers, Fashionable Feasts
S. Williams, 1985, 335 pp, hb $12.00
Scandinavian Cookbook
Culinary Arts, 1956, 68 pp, pb $3.00
Scandinavian Cookery for Americans
F. Brobeck, 1948, 341 pp, hb $10.00
School of Hope Cookbook
Mentally Retarded School, Ill., ca. 1960, 132 pp $2.50
Schoolmaster's View - Xmas Tea Cookies
Washington, 1957 .... $1.50

Salad Leaves
Ivanhoe Foods, Inc. - 1939

Savory Dishes
Kitchen Bouquet - Copyright 1916

Scientific Experiments You Can Eat
1972, 127 pp $3.50
Science of Food & Cookery
Anderson, 1938, 297 pp $12.00
Science of Food & Cookery
H. Anderson, ca. 1926, hb $18.00
Scientific Cooking with Scientific Methods
Craig, 1911 .... $12.00
Seafood Cookbook
Sunset, 1975, 96 pp, lf $4.00
Seafood with the Tang-o-the-Sea
Davis Fish Co., 31 pp, lf $3.00
Seafoods
Culinary Arts, 1955, 68 pp, pb $3.00
Sealtest Food Advisor
NY World's Fair, 1939, 15 pp, lf $4.50
Searchlight Cookbook
I. Migliario, 1952, 320 pp, hb $6.50
Sears Food Processor
Ca. 1970, 73 pp $2.00
Season To Taste - Spices . . . And How To Use Them
H.J. Mayer & Sons Co., Chicago, IL, 1939, 48 pp, pb $4.50
Seasonal Gifts From the Kitchen
E. Crumpacker, 1983, 1st edition $6.50
Seasoning Suggestions
Lea & Perrins, 1920 .... $5.00
Seasoning
French, 1951, 31 pp $2.50
Secrets of Chinese Cooking
Tsuifeng $5.00
Secrets of Good Cooking
Sister St. Mary, 1928, 309 pp $8.00
Secrets of the Jam Cupboard
Certo, 1932, 23 pp, pb $3.00
Selected Recipes That Keep Families Happy
McCormick Spice, 1928, 31 pp, pb $5.00
Selected Recipes from Hood College
1940 .... $5.00
Selection of Choice Recipes
Rumford, 1920, lf $1.00
Serve It and Sing
J. Platt, 1945, 70 pp, hb $5.00
Service Cookbook #1
I. Allen, 1933, hb $12.00
Service Cookbook #2
I. Allen, 1935 .... $6.00
Serving Food Attractively
F. Brobeck, pb $2.00

Season To Taste
Spices . . . And How To Use Them
H.J. Mayer & Sons Co. - Copyright 1939

Settlement Cookbook
S. Kander, 1938, 22nd edition, 623 pp, hb **$20.00**

Settlement Cookbook
S. Kander, 1949, 623 pp, hb **$14.00**

Several New Things Under Sun
Rumford, 1929 .... **$6.00**

Sexton Cookbook
J. Sexton, 1950, 432 pp, hb **$7.50**

Shaker Recipes for Cooks & Homemakers
W. Lassiter, 1959, 302 pp **$13.00**

Shoreline High PTA Cookbook
Washington, ca. 1950, 120 pp, pb **$4.00**

Shredded Wheat
1913 .... **$5.00**

Shrimp
Dunbar's shrimp, Barataria shrimp on back (see pg. 69) **$3.00**

Shumway's Handy Culture Book and Canning Recipes
Ca. 1950 .... **$1.00**

Simple Cooking for the Epicure
Campbell, 1955, 204 pp **$5.00**

Simplified Cooking
A. Peterson, Ill, 1926, 255 pp, hb **$18.00**

Simplified Hospitality
Servel, 1932, 47 pp, pb **$4.00**

Simply Delicious Meals in Minutes
Women's Day 1984, 112 pp, magazine **$1.00**

Simply Elegant Desserts
American Dairy Association, 23 pp, lf **$1.00**

Skillet Cookbook
Wesson, 1958, 64 pp **$2.50**

Slade's Cooking School
1906, 72 pp **$5.00**

Slade's Cooking School Recipes
Slade's spices, 1923 .... **$2.00**

Sleepy Eye Cookbook
Loaf of bread shaped **$35.00**

Sleepy Eye Flour Mills Cookbook
Old Sleepy eye in center **$300.00**

Sleepy Eye Milling Company
Old Sleepy Eye on right side w/bread **$150.00**

Slenderella Cookbook
M. Waldo, 1957, 335 pp, hb **$5.00**

Slices of Real Flavor
Armour, 16 pp, yellow cover, pb **$2.00**

Sloan's Y Hints and Up To Date Cookbook
1901, 47 pp, pb **$6.00**

Slumps, Grunts & Snickerdoodles
L. Perl, 125 pp, 1975, hb **$6.50**

Simplified Hospitality With Servel Hermetic
Copyright 1932, Serval Sales, Inc.

Smorgasbord & Scandinavian Cookery
  1948, 341 pp, hb **$8.00**
Smorgasbord Cookbook
  Coombs, 1949, 240 pp **$7.00**
Snacks and Refreshments
  Better Homes & Gardens, 1963, 61 pp, hb **$1.50**
Snoopy Doghouse Cookbook
  1979, 125 pp **$7.00**
Snow Drift Secrets
  Southern Cotton Oil, 1915, 46 pp, pb **$5.00**
So What if You Can't Chew
  P. Goldberg, 1980, 152 pp **$5.00**
Someone's in the Kitchen with Dinah
  D. Shore, 1971, 179 pp, hb **$8.00**
Something Different Dish
  M. Neil, ca. 1915, hb.. **$10.00**
Something's Always Cooking in Corning
  Corning Glass, ca. 1973 .... **$1.00**
Soufflé Spectaculars
  Kirshman, 1969, 48 pp, pb **$3.00**
Soup Recipes - 250
  Culinary Arts, 1954, 48 pp, pb **$4.50**
Sourdough Jack's Cookery
  J. Mabee, 1965, pb **$5.50**
South Carolina Cookbook
  Farm Women, 1954, 426 pp **$9.50**
South Florida Cookery
  A. Hawkes, 1964, signed **$7.00**
Southern Cookbook
  1956, 414 pp, pb **$4.00**
Southern Cooking
  Grosset, 1941 .... **$20.00**
Southern Pacific
  M. Medbgué and her Old Creole Cook, 1895, 78 pp **$18.00**
Souvenir from Kraft
  NY World's Fair, 1939, 3 leaflets **$8.50**
Soybeans for Health, Longevity & Economy
  Chen, 1956, 256 pp, hb... **$6.00**
Soyer's Cookery Book
  A. Soyer, 1959 .... **$6.50**
Speciality Cooking with Wine
  M. Wood, 1963, 224 pp **$4.00**
Speciality of the House - 100 Famous Cooks
  1955, hb **$5.00**
Spice Cookbook
  Day & Stucky, 1964, 597 pp... **$13.00**
Spices of Life
  B'nai B'rith, NJ, 1970, 309 pp, pb **$15.00**

Soufflé Spectaculars
By Irena Kirshman
1969

Sourdough Jack's Cookery
Copyright 1959 by "Sourdough Jack" Mabee

Spilling the Beans
J. Johnston, 1979, 234 pp, hb $6.00
Split-Level Cookbook
Gaeddert, 1967, 228 pp, hb $7.00
Spry
Can lid covers, recipes on back $1.00
Squash Cookbook
Y. Tarr, 1978, 223 pp, pb $4.00
St. Nicholas Flour Cookbook
Ca. 1915, lf $4.00
St. Augustine's Cookery
Flagler Hospital, FL, 1965, 20 pp, pb $2.50
St. Bart's Cookbook
St. Bartholomew's, NY, ca. 1960, 202 pp $5.00
St. John's Episcopal Church
NY, 1891, 78 pp $10.00
Staley's Selected Recipes
1935, 30 pp $3.00
Stalking the Wild Asparagus
E. Gibbons, 1962, 303 pp $5.50
Standard Cookbook for All Occasions
Lockhard, 1925 .... $18.00
Standard Family Cookbook
G. Wilkinson, 1959, 640 pp, hb $5.00
Standard Glass Churns
(19609) lf $1.00
Stillmeadow Cookbook
G. Taber, 1965, 335 pp, hb $42.00
Stina, H. Smith - Story of a Cook
1947, 242 pp $6.00
Stocking Up
Organic Garden, 1977, 532 pp, hb $12.50
Stonington Cooks & Cookery
CN, 1949, local, hb $10.00
Story of Chocolate and Cocoa
Hersey, 1936, pb $3.50
Story of Crisco
1914, pb $18.00
Success in Seasoning
Lea & Perrins, 1936, 47 pp, pb $3.00
Successful Preserving with Kold-pak Rubber Jars
1917, 16 pp $5.00
Sugar Spoon Recipes
Domino, 1962, 50 pp, hb $2.50
Summer Cookbook
L. Bruner, 1956 .... $5.00
Summertime Cookbook
Good Housekeeping, 1958, 68 pp, hb $2.00

Stocking Up
How to Preserve the Foods You Grow Naturally
By the Editors of Organic Gardening and Farming
Copyright 1977

Summertime is Coffee Time
A&P **$1.00**
Sun Maid Raisin Recipes
1923 .... **$7.00**
Sun Maid Raisins from Holland
8 pp, lf **$8.00**
Sunday Night Suppers
Culinary Arts, 1955, 68 pp, pb **$3.00**
Sunkist Recipes for Everyday
1933, 35 pp, lf **$2.25**
Sunkist Recipes, Orange-Lemons
1916, 64 pp, lf **$2.50**
Sunny Side of Life
Kellogg, 1934, pb **$5.00**
Sunset Barbeque Book
1942, Sunset, 91 pp, hb **$6.00**
Sunset Chefs of the West
1951, 219 pp, 1st edition **$10.00**
Sunset Cookbook for Entertaining
1968, 210 pp, hb **$4.50**
Sunset Kitchen Cabinet Volume 1
Volume 1, 1944, 128 pp, hb **$9.50**
Sunset Kitchen Cabinet Volume 2
1944, 128 pp, hb **$9.50**
Sunset Kitchen Cabinet Volume 3
1944, 128 pp, hb **$9.50**
Super Heroes Super Healthy Cookbook
M. Saltzman, 1981, 97 pp, hb **$8.00**
Suppers and Midnight Snacks
Bradshaw, 1969, 184 pp **$5.00**
Surplus Commodity Recipe Book
Parma, NY, 1986, 45 pp, pb **$2.00**
Susie's Cook Book
E. Smith, 1933, 317 pp **$7.00**
Swans Down Cake Book
1934, pb **$5.00**
Swedish Smorgasbord
A. Lampe, 1953, 78 pp **$2.50**
Sweet Ending
Dream Whip, 1974, 27 pp, lf **$1.50**
Sweet Talk
P. Penny, lf **$2.00**
Sweets from the Sweetest Little District
Eastern Star, ca. 1980, 70 pp **$2.50**
Sweets with All Sweet
M. Logan **$1.50**

Sunkist Recipes Oranges - Lemons
Copyright 1916 by California Fruit Growers Exchange

Tabasco - Its Romantic History
1961, 36 pp, lf $2.00
Table Decorations and Delicacies
H. Prices, 1914, hb $14.50
Taglienti Italian Cookbook
1955 .... $8.00
Take It Easy Before Dinner
R. Holberg, 1945, 98 pp $4.50
Talisman Italian Cook Book
A. Boni, 1958, 268 pp, hb $6.50
Taming of the C.A.N.D.Y.
V. Lansky, 1978, 140 pp $5.00
Tante Marie's French Pastry
146 pp, hb $8.50
Tassjara Cooking
Shambala, 1973, 54 pp, pb $2.00
Taste of Texas
1949, 303 pp $8.00
Taste of White House Cooking
A. Melick, lf $1.50
Tasty Dishes
Ponds, Ext, 1898, 48 pp, lf.. $8.00
Tea
I. Chalmers, 1978, 48 pp, pb $2.00
Teddy Bear Baking School
Fleischmann, 1906.. $25.00
Teenage Chef
J. Jackson, 1983, 86 pp, pb.. $1.50
Tempting Davis Recipes
Davis Baking Powder, 1925, 20 pp, pb $4.50
Tempting Good Luck Cookbook
Good Luck Margarine, 1932, 40 pp, pb................................ $4.00
Tempting Recipes for Waffle Irons
Gas & Electric shops, lf.. $1.00
Ten PM Cookbook
Good Housekeeping, 1958, 68 pp, pb $2.00
Tested and Proven Recipes
Mueller's, 1930, 40 pp, pb $6.50
Tested Recipes for Successful Baking
38 pp, pb, 6th edition.. $3.00
Text-book of Cooking
C. Greer, 1915, 431 pp.. $15.00
The Cup that Cheers
Tea Bureau, ca. 1950, 40 pp $4.00
There's Always Time to Cook Meat
1937, 40 pp $2.00

The Talisman Italian Cook Book
By Ada Boni
Crown Publishers, Inc. - 1958

Things You Have Always Wanted . . . Cooking
M. Mitchell, 1932, 78 pp $9.00
Thirty-cent Bread
McCann, 1917 .... $12.00
Thomas Jefferson's Cookbook
M. Kimball, 1949, 1st edition $15.00
Thoughts for Festive Foods
D. Wills, 1964, 687 pp, hb $8.00
Thoughts for Food - A Menu Aid
1938, 312 pp, 1st edition $10.00
Three Meals a Day
Metro Life, 16 pp, lf $2.00
Thrifty New Tips on a Grand Old Favorite - Heinz
1932, 20 pp $2.00
Time-Life Picture Cookbook
1958, 291 pp, hb $20.00
Time Reader's Book of Recipes
1949 .... $12.00
Time Tested Royal Recipes
31 pp, pb $5.00
Time to Entertain
C. Turgeon, 1976, 306 pp $1.50
Timely Baking Recipes with Swift Brand Lard
M. Logan, 35 pp $2.00
Timely Meat
National Livestock, 1945, 39 pp $2.00
Tinnay & Co. Cookbook
1907 .... $10.00
To the King's Taste
L. Sass, 1975, 144 pp, hb $4.00
Toll House Recipes
R. Wakdfidle, 1946, 275 pp $35.00
Tomatoes, Cheese and Anchovies Cookbook
Smith, 1967, 94 pp $3.00
Tonawanda Review Cookbook
Recipes of 500 women, 1883 .... $35.00
Too Hot to Cook Book
M. Ungerer, 1966, 376 pp, hb $3.50
Town Crier Flour Cookbook
1938 .... $4.00
Traditional Chinese Northern & Western Cuisine
E. Chen, 1976, 140 pp, signed $28.00
Trader Vic's Kitchen Kibitzer
1956 .... $10.00
Traditional Recipes for Christmas
Hardin, 1978, limited edition $60.00
Traditional Scots Recipes
J. Murray, 1972, 230 pp, hb $5.00

Traditional Chinese Northern and Western Cuisine
By Esther Chen

Traditional Southern and Eastern Cuisine
E. Chen, 1977, 358 pp, pb **$20.00**
Treadway Inns Cook Book
1958, 1st edition, signed **$10.00**
Treasure of Great Recipes
Price **$30.00**
Treasured Recipes of the Old South
Kimball, 1941, 21 pp, lf **$8.00**
Treasury of Outdoor Cooking
J. Beard, 1960, 282 pp **$12.50**
Treaties on Cake Making
Standard Brands, 1935, 468 pp **$12.50**
Tried and True
Trinity Church, Niles, MI, 1907, 228 pp, pb **$12.00**
Tried Receipts
1909, 115 pp, hb **$15.50**
Tried Temptations
E. Haines, 1926, 73 pp **$8.50**
Tropical Native Cook
Marathon Garden Club, FL, 1977, pb **$3.50**
Twelve Days of Christmas Cookbook
S. Huntley, 1965, 143 pp **$6.00**
Twentieth Century Cookbook
1921, 164 pp **$18.00**
Tyson Baking Book
Marion, 1916 .... **$15.00**

ᚙ **U** ᚙ

Uncle Sam's Cookbook
C. Woods, 1904, leather bound **$12.50**
Union Gas & Electric Company Cookbook
Cincinnati, 1907, 168 pp, pb **$10.00**
United States Regional Cookbook
Berolzheimer, 1939, 752 pp, hb **$6.00**
United States Regional Cookbook
R. Berolzheimer, 1941 .... **$15.00**
Universal Cookbook
With advice to Housewives, 1923, 724 pp **$25.00**
Universal Cookbook
J. Taylor, 1888, 185 pp **$12.00**
University Garden Club
Rochester, NY, 1937 .... **$3.50**
Unprejudiced Palate
A. Pellegrini, 1949, 235 pp **$6.50**
Unusual Old World Recipes
Ca. 1960, 46 pp, lf **$2.00**
Up-to-date Waitress
J. Hill, 1906, pb **$15.00**
Useful Facts
Dr. Miles **$2.00**

Vaughn Feed Store - Vegetable Cookbook
1919 ....$7.50
VB Brand Old Fashion Apple Sauce
Lf $3.50
Vegetable Cookery
M. Waldo, 1962, 186 pp, pb $3.00
Vegetable for Health
Stokely, 1929, 30 pp, lf...$5.50
Vegetables Money Can't Buy
N. Bubel, 188 pp, hb $2.50
Vegetables - 250 Ways to Serve
Culinary Arts, 1954, pb $4.50
Vegetables
Good Housekeeping, 1958, 68 pp, pb $2.00
Vegetarian Cookbook
1922 ....$3.00
Vegetarian Epicure
A. Thomas, 1972, 262 recipes $6.00
Veritable Cuisine de Famille
T. Marie, Paris, 1920 ....$30.00
Vermont Maple Recipes
1952, 87 pp $5.00
Victory Cookbook War Time Edition
R. Berolzheimer, ca. 1940, 880 pp, hb $15.00
Victory Cookbook
Lysol, ca. 1936, lf..$3.00
Victory Demands More Canning
Kerr, 22 pp, lf $2.00
Victory Garden Cookbook
M. Morash, 1982, 371 pp, pb..$17.95
Victory Meat Extender
National Livestock, WWII, 39 pp, lf..$3.50
Viennese Cookbook
Rhode, 1951, 260 pp $9.50
Viennese Cuisine - I Love NY
Bond, 1977, 160 pp $7.00
Virginia Housewife Methodical Cook
Randolph, 1831, 1st. edition $300.00
Visions of Sugarplums
Sunsweet, 1959, lf...$2.00
Vital Foods for Total Health
Jensen, 1955, 382 pp, pb $5.00
Vital Vegetables
I. Allen, 1928, 466 pp, signed $30.00
Vitality Demands Energy
General Mills, 1934, 50 pp, pb $64.00

Vision of Sugarplums
29 delightful ways to serve Sunsweet Prunes
Copyright 1959

The VEGETABLE BOOK

Being a collection of tested recipes of fresh and canned vegetables-showing their dietetic value and giving sensible methods of cookery and service

ORIGINATED AND PUBLISHED BY
WOMAN'S WORLD MAGAZINE CO. INC.
CHICAGO, U.S.A.

The Vegetable Cook
Originated and Published by
Woman's World Magazine Co., Inc. Copyright 1928

Wallace Hostess Book
W. Fales, Wallace Silver, 1922, 36 pp, pb **$12.00**
Walter Baker Choice Recipes
1914, lf **$12.00**
Walter Baker Company
1925 .... **$8.00**
Want Something Different
1931 .... **$3.00**
War Time Spreads and Sandwich Fillings
NY, 1940 .... **$1.00**
War-Time Cook and Health Book
L. Pinkham, WWI, 32 pp **$5.00**
Waring Blender Cookbook
S. Schur, 1958, 128 pp **$1.00**
Warnes Model Cookery & Housekeeping Book
Jewry **$35.00**
Wartime Cookbook
A. Baley, 1943, 128 pp **$3.00**
Washburn Recipes
Moscow, Idaho, 1948, 31 pp, lf **$2.00**
Washington Herald Recipe Book
1940 .... **$10.00**
Waterless Cooker Recipe Book
1927, 11 pp **$8.00**
Watkins Almanac 1938
288 pp, pb **$7.00**
Watkins Almanac
45th year, Grams and Gramps, pb **$12.50**
Watkins Almanac
49th 1916, pb **$10.00**
Watkins Almanac
51st 1918, pb **$8.00**
Watkins Almanac Home Doctor and Cookbook
Watkins, 1932, 92 pp, pb **$4.50**
Watkins Cook Book
1938, 288 pp, hb **$7.00**
Watkins Cookbook
1903, 46 pp **$15.00**
Watkins Cookbook
1936, Allen, 192 pp, hb **$18.00**
Watkins Salad Cookbook
B. Allen, 1946, 251 pp, hb **$15.00**
Way to a Man's Heart
Settlement Cookbook, 1930, 624, hb **$9.00**
Ways of Cooking
Rombauer & Becker, 1983, 916 pp, hb **$13.00**

War-Time Cook and Health Book
Printed at the request of the
Department of Food Conservation
July 23, 1917

Watkins Almanac Home Doctor & Cookbook
1915 - 48th Year
The J.R. Watkins Medical Company

Weight Watcher's 365-Day Menu Cookbook
1981, 343 pp **$4.00**
Well Dressed Desserts
Cool Whip, 16 pp, pb **$1.00**
Wesson Oil Salad Time
1924, pb **$4.25**
Western Cookery
K. Morris, 1936, 48 pp, pb **$4.50**
Westinghouse Sugar & Spice Cookbook
1951, lf **$3.00**
What Actors Eat
R. Lease, 1939 .... **$8.50**
What Shall I Cook Today
Spry, pb **$5.00**
What To Eat & How To Cook It
P. Blott, 1865 .... **$70.00**
What To Eat & How To Prepare It
Monaghan, 1922 .... **$10.00**
What to Eat
C. Brown, Prudential Life, 15 pp, vegtable basket cover, pb **$2.00**
What to Serve
YWCA, 1933, 44 pp, pb **$2.00**
What Will We Eat Today?
Press Cookery, Culinary Arts, 1949, 194 pp **$6.00**
What You Can Do With Jell-o
1933, 26 pp **$3.00**
What's Cooking in Our National Parks
H. Chapman, 1973, 250 pp, pb **$4.00**
What's Cookin' in Morton
Fire Company, NY, 1948, 44 pp, pb **$6.50**
What's Cookin'
J. Bailey, 1949 .... **$12.00**
What's Cooking at Columbia
War Relief, 1942 .... **$3.00**
What's Cooking in Parma, NY
1981, 61 pp, pb **$4.50**
Wheatena
1906, lf **$3.00**
When Meals Were Meals
M. Dickinson, 1967, 185 pp, pb **$7.50**
When You Bake with Yeast
Fleischmann's, 32 pp, lf **$2.00**
When You Entertain
Coca Cola, 1932, 124 pp, hb **$25.00**
White House Cookbook in German
Gillette, 1899, 649 pp **$25.00**
White House Cookbook
1889, F. Gillette **$100.00**

White House Cookbook
  1894 .... **$95.00**
White House Cookbook
  1899, 590 pp, hb **$40.00**
White House Cookbook
  1902, hb **$80.00**
White House Cookbook
  1903, hb **$40.00**
White House Cookbook
  1905, enlarged, 590 pp, Roosevelt, hb **$30.00**
White House Cookbook
  1911, hb **$42.00**
White House Cookbook
  1923, 533 pp, hb **$45.00**
White House Cookbook
  1926, 680 pp, hb **$50.00**
White House Cookbook
  1960, 516 pp, hb **$20.00**
White House Cookbook
  1967, 287 pp, hb, Kennedy **$20.00**
Who Says We Can't Cook
  Women's National Press, 1955, 176 pp, pb.................. **$12.00**
Whole Earth Cookbook
  S. Cadwallader, 1972, 120 pp **$2.00**
Whole Food for the Whole Family
  Johnson, 1981, 340 pp, pb.. **$4.00**
Whole Wheat Way to Better Meals
  Shredded Wheat, 1940, pb.. **$5.00**
Wholly Scrumptures
  Webster Baptist Church, NY, 290 pp, pb **$5.50**
Wilcolator Cookbook
  31 pp, pb, green cover.. **$1.50**
Wild Mushroom Recipes
  C. Eberly, 63 pp, lf.. **$3.00**
Wild Plums in Brandy
  S. Boorman, 1969, 194 pp **$7.00**
Wilder's Bitters Cookbook
  .... **$4.50**
Wilderness Cooking
  Berglund, 1973, 192 pp **$11.00**
Wilken's Family Home Cooking Album
  1935, pb **$12.00**
Williamsburg Art of Cookry . . .
  H. Bullock, 1942, hb **$12.00**
Williamsburg Cookbook
  1975, pb **$5.00**
Wills Reality presents Their Famous Cookbook
  1986, 128 pp **$2.00**

Wilson's Meat Cookery
E. Wright, 1922, 46 pp, pb **$6.00**
Wind in Willows Country Cookbook
A. Boxer, 1983, 117 pp **$5.50**
Wine Cookbook
The Browns, 1934, 460 pp, hb **$12.50**
Wine Lover's Cookbook
1953, 197 pp **$4.00**
Wines & Spirits
W. Massee, 1961, 387 pp, hb **$7.50**
Winston Cook Book
H. Cramp, 1922, 507 pp, hb **$8.00**
Winter Kitchen
Kent, 1962, 326 pp, hb **$4.00**
WIRQ Cookbook
1974, 45 pp, pb **$2.50**
Wise Encyclopedia of Cookery
1948, 1,337 pp, hb **$17.50**
Wise Encyclopedia of Cooking
W. Wise, 1971, 1,329 pp, hb **$8.00**
With Wesson Oil
1926, 35 pp, pb **$2.00**
Woman's Institute of Domestic Arts & Science . . . Meats
1918, magazine **$3.50**
Woman's National Republican Club of Chicago
1931, hb **$6.00**
Woman's World Calendar Cookbook
I. Allen, 1922, 96 pp **$8.50**
Woman's Day Cookie Cookbook
Pb **$2.00**
Woman's Day Encyclopedia of Cookery
1965, 12 volumes **$25.00**
Woman's Exchange Cookbook
M. Palmer, 1894, 511 pp, hb **$55.00**
Woman's Favorite Cookbook
A. Gregory, 1902, 511 pp, hb **$40.00**
Woman's Home Companion
Kirk, 1955 .... **$25.00**
Woman's Home
D. Kirk, 1946, 951 pp, hb **$10.00**
Woman's World Cookbook
1939, 800 pp **$12.00**
Woman's World Cookery Calendar
1922, 66 pp, pb **$6.00**
Women's Institute Library of Cookery
1919, hb, set of 5 .... **$25.00**
Women's Institute Library of Cookery
1928, 53 pp **$3.00**

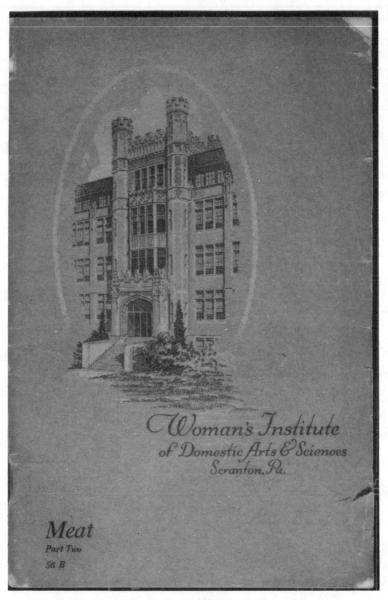

Woman's Institute of Domestic Arts

of Domestic Arts & Sciences

Scranton, Pa.

Meat

Part Two

58 B

Woman's Institute of Domestic Arts & Sciences
Scranton, PA
Meats Part 2 - Copyright 1918

Women's Republican Club of Irondequoit Cookbook
Rochester, NY, M. Schuchart $3.00
Women's Temperance Kitchen Wall Cookbook
1888, 27 pp $45.00
Women's World Salad Book
1929 .... $10.00
Wonder Bread Cookbook
1930, pb $4.00
Wonderful World of Freezer Cooking
H. Quat, 1964, 224 pp, hb $1.50
Wonderful World of Welch's
Welch's Grape, 96 pp, pb $3.00
Wonderland of Homemade Jams and Jellies
1974, 32 pp, pb $1.00
Wood Stove Cookry - At Home on the Range
1977, 208 pp, pb $3.00
Worchester Cookbook
Worchester Salt, J. Hill, 32 pp, pb $2.00
Working Girls Must Eat
H. Young, 1938, 208 pp, hb $8.00
Working Wives', Salaried or Other, Cookbook
T. Zavin, 1963, 162 pp, hb $5.00
World Famous Chefs
F. Naylor, 1940 .... $50.00
World's Fair Cookbook
1982, official, Knoxville, TN, pb $8.00
World's Fair Menu Recipe Book
San Francisco, J. Lehner, 1915 .... $39.00
World's Modern Cookbook for the Busy Woman
M. Claire, 1942, 312 pp, hb $7.00

Yankee Cookbook
I. Wolcott, 1939, 398 pp **$8.00**

Yankee Magazine's Favorite New England Recipes
Stamm, 1972, 303 pp **$10.50**

Year Round Holiday Cookbook
Huntley, 1969, 214 pp, hb **$6.00**

Year Round Recipes
Dairlea, 33 pp **$2.00**

Yeast Baking and Your Gold Medal
1963, 20 pp, lf **$1.50**

Yeast Foam Recipes
Northwestern Yeast, ca. 1900 .... **$3.00**

Yes Homemade Banana Recipes
Standard Fruit, 1929, 22 pp, lf **$5.00**

Yorktown Cookbook
Local, Virginia, 1957, 85 pp, pb **$3.00**

You Are What You Eat
V. Lindlahr, 1940, 128 pp, pb **$2.00**

You Can't Eat Mt. Rainier
Speidel, 1955, 134 pp, hb **$7.00**

Young American Cookbook
1938, 274 pp, hb **$6.00**

Young Housekeeper or Thoughts on Food & Cookery
Alcott, 1838, 424 pp **$50.00**

Your Frigidaire Recipes
General Motors, 1945, 36 pp, pb **$3.00**

Your Future in the Tea Cup
Lipton, 1935 .... **$3.00**

Your Home Cook Book
Dane, 1929, 1st edition **$10.00**

Your Share
Betty Crocker, 1943, 48 pp, pb **$3.25**

Your Victory Lunchbox
G. Buchholz, 50 pp **$1.00**

Yul Brynner Cookbook
1983 .... **$15.00**

Zane Grey Cookbook
B. Rieger, 1976 .... **$20.00**

Zen Cookery
SHWA, 1966, 79 pp, pb **$3.50**

You Can't Eat Mount Rainier
The Seattle Guide to Restaurants, Recipes and Food
By William C. Speidel, Jr.
Copyright 1955

the philosophy of oriental culture   vol. I

zen cookery

practical macrobiotics

Zen Cookery
Practical Macrobiotics
Copyright 1966

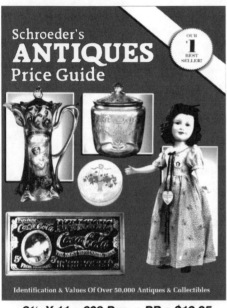